About the author

Douglas William Jerrold (1803–1857) was the son of a theatre manager and claimed to have appeared on stage with Edmund Kean as a child. He joined the Navy at the age of ten and served in a ship which brought back the wounded from Waterloo. After a spell working in a printer's office, he began writing plays of which *Black-ey'd Susan* and *The Bride of Ludgate* were his greatest successes. He became a contributor to many periodicals including *Blackwood's* and the *Athenaeum* and was a key player during the early years of *Punch*, writing under the pseudonym "Q". He also became editor of a succession of publications including *Douglas Jerrold's Shilling Magazine*, and *Douglas Jerrold's Weekly Newspaper*. When *Punch* published *Mrs Caudle's Curtain Lectures* in 1845 it was an immediate success both in Britain and on the Continent. He thrived at the centre of London's literary life and numbered Dickens and Thackeray among his friends.

Mrs. Caudle's Curtain Lectures

Prion Humour Classics

* for copyright reasons these titles are not available in the USA or Canada in the Prion edition.

Mrs. Caudle's Curtain Lectures

Douglas Jerrold

with a new introduction by

PETER ACKROYD

This collection published in 2000 by
Prion Books Limited,
Imperial Works,
Perren Street,
London NW5 3ED
www.prionbooks.com

First published by Punch in 1845
Introduction copyright © 2000 Peter Ackroyd

Cataloguing in Publication Data
A catalogue record for this book is available
from the British Library

ISBN 1-85375-400-5

Jacket design by David Butler
Printed and bound in Great Britain
by Creative Print & Design, Wales

Contents

Introduction

by PETER ACKROYD

The titles of these "lectures" are enough, and more than enough, to set the scene—"Mrs Caudle 'Wishes to Know if They're Going to the Sea-Side, or Not, this Summer—That's All'", "Mr Caudle Has Not Acted 'Like a Husband' at the Wedding Dinner", "Mrs Caudle 'Has Been Told' that Caudle Has 'Taken to Play' at Billiards". Job Caudle, mid-Victorian toy man and doll merchant, retires to bed only to be confronted by his wife in unforgiving mood; she has waited all day, and this is her opportunity to unload all her complaints and grievances into the unwilling and sometimes unreceptive ear of her husband. She is what was once known as a 'scold' or 'nag', but one whose tone of majestic reproof has few equals in nineteenth century literature. "Yes, Mr Caudle, I knew it would come to this. I said it would…It's all very well for you…I know I'm right…I should like to know…Don't tell me…I only wish my time was to come over again".

She complains that he has lent five pounds to a friend, that he has been drinking brandy and water until one in the morning, that he has smoked tobacco in a tavern, that he has smiled at their maid. She wants a chaise, a cottage in the country, and her mother to share the house with them. It may all seem very incorrect and unenlightened at the beginning of the twenty-first century, but it represents a type of English humour that is as old as the language itself and as recent as the latest situation comedy on television.

Douglas Jerrold himself is now almost forgotten, but he was one of the most popular writers of his period. He was born in 1803, the son of an itinerant actor and as a child he himself played upon the stage. These dramatic origins, however humble, are evident in Margaret Caudle's highly theatrical monologues. He became a midshipman but, hating service at sea, he set himself up a writer of plays and farces. His first real dramatic success was the melodrama, *Black-ey'd Susan*, but he soon became known also as a crusading radical journalist and polemicist: like many of his contemporaries, he was a man of inexhaustible talent and inventiveness.

He was small, with a very large head and very sharp features; he wore his hair long, and at moments of more than usual excitement he tossed it back "like a lion does with its mane". He was filled with an intense nervous energy and was afflicted, according to a contemporary, with a "peculiar restlessness of eye, speech and demeanour". And, as this volume testifies, he could also be very funny. When asked with whom his wife was dancing he replied, "Some member of the Humane Society". When asked why one particular playwright had such dirty hands he said, "From his habit of constantly putting them up to his face".

He was one of the "Punch brotherhood" or, in the words of detractors of that recently established journal, "one of those Punch people". Mrs Caudle herself emerged in all her glory in that periodical; the first "lecture" appeared in the issue of 4 January 1845, and at once it made the nation laugh. An historian of Punch has observed that "it created a national furore and set the whole country laughing and talking. Other nations soon took up the conversation and the laughter and 'Mrs Caudle' passed into the popular mind and took a permanent place in the language in an incredibly short space of time".

Jerrold's son has revealed that his father was often compelled to dictate the latest 'lecture' while lying on a bed incapacitated by rheumatism; this makes the cogent point that the funniest writing can come from the most despondent or infirm writer. And, as Blanchard Jerrold relates, Mrs Caudle was "welcomed by the laughing thousands". What were the reasons for her success? Blanchard Jerrold believes it to lie in the secret hostilities of Victorian social life, where everyone could point the finger at the next door neighbour's wife as a true copy of the nagging Mrs Caudle.

But her origins lie deeper than that. The husband's name of Job is appropriate and perhaps significant, since the figure of the scold has biblical antecedents. In the English mystery plays Noah's wife has a temperament and role very similar to that of Mrs Caudle, and the tradition of lampooning females in England has continued ever since. She is Mrs Gamp; she is Mrs Malaprop; she is the wife of Andy Capp. Or, as Douglas Jerrold put it, "she was not a woman to wear chains without shaking them". As Margaret Caudle herself says, on the subject of sewing shirt buttons, "It's what people have always told me it would come to—and now, the buttons have opened my eyes! But the whole world shall know of your cruelty, Mr Caudle. After the wife I've been to you." And so she goes on, in a veritable stream of consciousness not unlike the monologues which music-hall artists were soon to perform upon the stage. If there is one successor to Mrs Caudle, it is Dan Leno in his female incarnations. But she also resembles Dickens's female creations, drowning not waving in the sea of their own verbosity.

One of the incidental delights in reading these tirades lies in the insights which they reveal into the nature of Victorian life, with the references to fire-rates and pickled cabbage, the Union and the mania for railway shares, the "pot-companion" and the sponging house. When a cottage out of town is mentioned, "genteel" Brixton happens to be the favoured spot closely followed by Balham Hill; Battersea is "too low", in social terms, and Muswell Hill "too high". When Job Caudle ventures to mention Gravesend as the possible site for a holiday, his wife of fourteen years has a magnificent retort—"Gravesend! You might as well empty a salt cellar in the New River and call that the sea-side". The social customs are interesting. Some such as the Freemasons have survived, but others like Greenwich Fair have gone for ever. It was clearly a matter of pride that the husband did not own a house-key, presumably on the grounds that he might then return at all hours. What is clear however is that the role of paterfamilias was an ambiguous one. Contrary to popular belief, the Victorian male was not necessarily masterful and domineering at all, rather, as Mr Caudle himself admits, "man is frail—and woman is strong".

Mrs Caudle's Curtain Lectures might almost be described as a Victorian *Arabian Nights* except, alas, in this case the ending is not deferred for ever. A psychologist might argue that the talk before sleep was some kind of substitute for sex—hence the note of barely restrained hysteria—if it were not for the fact that there also seems to be an unlimited supply of children. But analysis is useless in the face of a phenomenon such as Margaret Caudle. It need only be stated that, with his creation, Douglas Jerrold has earned a place with Oscar Wilde and Mark Twain as one of the great comic geniuses of his century. He died young, at the age of fifty four, but Mrs Caudle is ageless.

Preface

It has happened to the writer that two, or three, or ten, or twenty gentlewomen, have asked him—and asked in various notes of wonder, pity, and reproof—

"What could have made you think of Mrs. Caudle? How could such a thing have entered any man's mind?"

There are subjects that seem like raindrops to fall upon a man's head, the head itself having nothing to do with the matter. The result of no train of thought, there is the picture, the statue, the book, wafted, like the smallest seed, into the brain to feed upon the soil, such as it may be, and grow there. And this was no doubt, the accidental cause of the literary sowing, and expansion— unfolding like a night-flower—of MRS. CAUDLE.

But let a jury of gentlewomen decide.

It was a thick, black wintry afternoon, when the writer stopt in the front of the play-ground of a suburban school. The ground swarmed with boys full of the Saturday's holiday. The earth seemed roofed with the oldest lead; and the wind came, sharp as Shylock's knife, from the Minories. But those happy boys ran and jumped, and hopped and shouted, and—unconscious men in miniature!—in their own world of frolic, had no thought of the full-length men they would some day become; drawn out into grave citizenship; formal, respectable, responsible. To them the sky was of any or all colours; and for that keen east-wind—if it was called the east-wind—cutting the shoulder-blades of old, old men of forty—they in their immortality of boyhood had the redder faces, and the nimbler blood for it.

And the writer, looking dreamily into that play-ground, still mused on the robust jollity of those little fellows, to whom the tax-gatherer was as yet a rarer animal than baby hippopotamus. Heroic boyhood, so ignorant of the future in the knowing enjoyment of the present! And the writer, still dreaming and musing, and still following no distinct line of thought, there struck upon him, like notes of sudden household music, these words—CURTAIN LECTURES.

One moment there was no living object save those racing, shouting boys; and the next, as though a white dove had alighted on the pen-hand of the writer, there was—MRS. CAUDLE.

Ladies of the jury, are there not then some subjects of letters that mysteriously assert an effect without any discoverable cause? Otherwise, wherefore should the thought of CURTAIN LECTURES grow from a school-ground—wherefore, among a crowd of holiday schoolboys, should appear MRS. CAUDLE?

For the LECTURES themselves, it is feared they must be given up as a farcical desecration of a solemn time-honoured privilege; it may be, exercised once in a lifetime,—and that once having the effect of a hundred repetitions: as Job lectured his wife. And Job's wife, a certain Mohammedan writer delivers, having committed a fault in her love to her husband, he swore that on his recovery he would deal her a hundred stripes. Job got well, and his heart was touched and taught by the tenderness to keep his vow, and still to chastise his helpmate; for he smote her once with a palm-branch having a hundred leaves.

D.J.

Foreword

Poor Job Caudle was one of the few men whom Nature, in her casual bounty to women, sends into the world as patient listeners. He was, perhaps, in more respects than one, all ears. And these ears, Mrs. Caudle—his lawful, wedded wife, as she would ever and anon impress upon him, for she was not a woman to wear chains without shaking them—took whole and sole possession of. They were her entire property; as expressly made to convey to Caudle's brain the stream of wisdom that continually flowed from the lips of his wife, as was the tin funnel through which Mrs. Caudle in vintage time bottled her elder wine. There was, however, this difference between the wisdom and the wine. The wine was always sugared: the wisdom never. It was expressed crude from the heart of Mrs. Caudle; who, doubtless, trusted to the sweetness of her husband's disposition to make it agree with him.

Philosophers have debated whether morning or night is most conducive to the strongest and clearest moral impressions. The Grecian sage confessed that his labours smelt of the lamp. In like manner, did Mrs. Caudle's wisdom smell of the rushlight. She knew that her husband was too much distracted by his business as toyman and doll-merchant to digest her lessons in the broad day. Besides, she could never make sure of him: he was always liable to be summoned to the shop. Now from eleven at night until seven in the morning, there was no retreat for him. He was compelled to lie and listen. Perhaps there was little magnanimity in this on the part of Mrs. Caudle; but in marriage, as in war, it is permitted to take every advantage of the enemy. Besides, Mrs. Caudle copied very ancient and classic authority. Minerva's bird, the very wisest thing in feathers, is silent all the day. So was Mrs. Caudle. Like the owl, she hooted only at night.

Mr. Caudle was blessed with an indomitable con-stitution. One fact will prove the truth of this. He lived thirty years with Mrs. Caudle, surviving her. Yes, it took thirty years for Mrs. Caudle to lecture and dilate upon the joys, griefs, duties, and vicissitudes comprised within that seemingly small circle—the wedding-ring. We say, seemingly small; for the thing, as viewed by the vulgar, naked eye, is a tiny hoop made for the third feminine finger. Alack! like the ring of Saturn, for good or evil it circles a whole world. Or to take a less gigantic figure, it compasses a vast region; it may be Arabia Felix, and it may be Arabia Petrea.

A lemon-hearted cynic might liken the wedding-ring to an ancient Circus, in which wild animals clawed one another for the sport of lookers-on. Perish the hyper-bole! We would rather compare it to an elfin ring, in which dancing fairies made the sweetest music for infirm humanity.

Manifold are the uses of rings. Even swine are tamed by them. You will see a vagrant, hilarious, devastating porker—a full-blooded fellow that would bleed into many, many fathoms of black pudding—you will see him, escaped from his proper home, straying in a neighbour's garden. How he tramples upon the heart's-ease: how, with quivering snout, he roots up lilies—odoriferous bulbs! Here he gives a reckless snatch at thyme and marjoram—and here he munches violets and gillyflowers. At length the marauder is detected, seized by his owner, and driven, beaten home. To make the porker less dangerous, it is determined that he shall be *ringed*. The sentence is pronounced—execution ordered. Listen to his screams!

> "Would you not think the knife was in his throat?
> And yet they're only boring through his nose!"

Hence, for all future time, the porker behaves himself with a sort of forced propriety—for in either nostril he carries a ring. It is, for the greatness of humanity, a saddening thought, that sometimes men must be treated no better than pigs.

But Mr. Job Caudle was not of these men. Marriage to him was not made a necessity. No; for him—call it if you will a happy chance—a golden accident. It is, however, enough for us to know that he was married; and was therefore made the recipient of a wife's wisdom. Mrs. Caudle, like Mahomet's dove, con-tinually pecked at the good man's ears; and it is a happiness to learn from what he left behind that he had hived all her sayings in his brain; and further, that he employed the mellow evening of his life to put such sayings down, that, in due season they might be enshrined in imperishable type.

When Mr. Job Caudle was left in this briary world

without his daily guide and nocturnal monitress, he was in the ripe fulness of fifty-two. For three hours at least after he went to bed—such slaves are we to habit—he could not close an eye. His wife still talked at his side. True it was, she was dead and decently interred. His mind—it was a comfort to know it—could not wander on this point; this he knew. Nevertheless, his wife was with him. The Ghost of her Tongue still talked as in the life; and again and again did Job Caudle hear the monitions of by-gone years. At times, so loud, so lively, so real were the sounds, that Job, with a cold chill, doubted if he were really widowed. And then with the movement of an arm, a foot, he would assure himself that he was alone in his holland. Nevertheless, the talk continued. It was terrible to be thus haunted by a voice: to have advice, commands, remonstrance, all sorts of saws and adages still poured upon him, and no visible wife. Now did the voice speak from the curtains; now from the tester; and now did it whisper to Job from the very pillow that he pressed. "It's a dreadful thing that her tongue should walk in this manner," said Job, and then he thought confusedly of exorcism, or at least of counsel from the parish priest.

Whether Job followed his own brain, or the wise direction of another, we know not. But he resolved every night to commit to paper one curtain lecture of his late wife. The employment would, possibly, lay the ghost that haunted him. It was her dear tongue that cried for justice, and when thus satisfied, it might possibly rest in quiet. And so it happened. Job faithfully chronicled all his late wife's lectures; the ghost of her tongue was thenceforth silent, and Job slept all his after nights in peace.

When Job died, a small packet of papers was found inscribed as follows:

"Curtain Lectures delivered in the course of Thirty
Years by Mrs. Margaret Caudle, and suffered by
Job, her Husband."

That Mr. Caudle had his eye upon the future printer, is made pretty probable by the fact that in most places he had affixed the text—such text for the most part arising out of his own daily conduct—to the lecture of the night. He had also, with an instinctive knowledge of the dignity of literature, left a bank-note of very fair amount with the manuscript. Following our duty as editor, we trust we have done justice to both documents.

Lecture I

Mr. Caudle Has Lent Five Pounds to a Friend

"You ought to be very rich, Mr. Caudle. I wonder who'd lend you five pounds? But so it is: a wife may work and may slave! Ha, dear! the many things that might have been done with five pounds. As if people picked up money in the street! But you always were a fool, Mr. Caudle! I've wanted a black satin gown these three years, and that five pounds would have entirely bought it. But it's no matter how I go—not at all. Everybody says I don't dress as becomes your wife—and I don't; but what's that to you, Mr. Caudle? Nothing. Oh no! you can have fine feelings for everybody but those belonging to you. I wish people knew you, as I do—that's all. You like to be called liberal—and your poor family pays for it.

"All the girls want bonnets, and where they're to come from I can't tell. Half five pounds would have bought 'em—but now they must go without. Of course, *they* belong to you: and anybody but your own flesh and blood, Mr. Caudle!

"The man called for the water-rate to-day; but I should like to know how people are to pay taxes, who throw away five pounds to every fellow that asks them?

"Perhaps you don't know that Jack, this morning,

1

MR CAUDLE LENDS FIVE POUNDS TO A FRIEND.

knocked his shuttle-cock through his bed-room window. I was going to send for the glazier to mend it; but after you lent that five pounds I was sure we couldn't afford it. Oh, no! the window must go as it is; and pretty weather for a dear child to sleep with a broken window. He's got a cold already on his lungs, and I shouldn't at all wonder if that broken window settled him. If the dear boy dies, his death will be upon his father's head; for I'm sure we can't now pay to mend windows. We might though, and do a good many more things, too, if people didn't throw away their five pounds.

"Next Tuesday the fire-insurance is due. I should like to know how it's to be paid? Why, it can't be paid at all! That five pounds would have more than done it—and now, insurance is out of the question. And there never were so many fires as there are now. I shall never close my eyes all night—but what's that to you, so people can call you liberal, Mr. Caudle? Your wife and children may all be burnt alive in their beds—as all of us to a certainty shall be, for the insurance *must* drop. And after we've insured for so many years! But how, I should like to know, are people to insure who make ducks and drakes of their five pounds?

"I did think we might go to Margate this summer. There's poor little Caroline, I'm sure she wants the sea. But no, dear creature! she must stop at home—all of us must stop at home—she'll go into a consumption, there's no doubt of that; yes—sweet little angel!—I've made up my mind to lose her, *now*. The child might have been saved; but people can't save their children and throw away their five pounds too.

"I wonder where poor little Mopsy is? While you were lending that five pounds, the dog ran out of the shop. You know, I never let it go into the street, for fear it should be bit by some mad dog, and come home and bite all the children. It wouldn't now at all astonish me if the animal was to come back with the hydrophobia, and give it to all the family. However, what's your family to you, so you can play the liberal creature with five pounds?

"Do you hear that shutter, how it's banging to and fro? Yes—I know what it wants as well as you; it wants a new fastening. I was going to send for the blacksmith to-day, but now it's out of the question: *now* it must bang of nights, since you've thrown away five pounds.

"Ha! there's the soot falling down the chimney. If I hate the smell of anything, it's the smell of soot. And you know it; but what are my feelings to you? *Sweep the chimney*! Yes, it's all very fine to say, sweep the chimney—but how are chimneys to be swept—how are they to be paid for by people who don't take care of their five pounds?

"Do you hear the mice running about the room? *I* hear them. If they were to drag only you out of bed, it would be no matter. *Set a trap for them*! Yes, it's easy enough to say—set a trap for 'em. But how are people to afford mouse-traps, when every day they lose five pounds?

"Hark! I'm sure there's a noise down stairs. It wouldn't at all surprise me if there were thieves in the house. Well, it *may* be the cat; but thieves are pretty sure to come in some night. There's a wretched fastening to the back door; but these are not times to afford bolts and bars, when people won't take care of their five pounds.

"Mary Anne ought to have gone to the dentist's to-morrow. She wants three teeth taken out. Now, it can't be done. Three teeth that quite disfigure the child's mouth. But there they must stop, and spoil the sweetest face that was ever made. Otherwise, she'd have been a wife for a lord. Now, when she grows up, who'll have her? Nobody. We shall die, and leave her alone and unprotected in the world. But what do you care for that? Nothing; so you can squander away five pounds."

"And thus," comments Caudle, "according to my wife, she—dear soul!—couldn't have a satin gown—the girls couldn't have new bonnets—the water-rate must stand over—Jack must get his death through a broken window—our fire-insurance couldn't be paid, so that we should all fall victims to the devouring element—we couldn't go to Margate, and Caroline would go to an early grave—the dog would come home and bite us all mad—the shutter would go banging for ever—the soot would always fall—the mice never let us have a wink of sleep—thieves be always breaking in the house—our dear Mary Anne be for ever left an unprotected maid—and with other evils falling upon us, all, all because I would go on lending five pounds!"

Lecture II

Mr. Caudle Has Been at a Tavern with a Friend, and "Is Enough to Poison a Woman" with Tobacco-Smoke

"I'm sure I don't know who'd be a poor woman! I don't know who'd tie themselves up to a man, if they knew only half they'd have to bear. A wife must stay at home, and be a drudge, whilst a man can go anywhere. It's enough for a wife to sit like Cinderella by the ashes, whilst her husband can go drinking and singing at a tavern. *You never sing*? How do I know you never sing? It's very well for you to say so; but if I could hear you, I dare say you're among the worst of 'em.

"And now, I suppose, it will be the tavern every night? If you think I'm going to sit up for you, Mr. Caudle, you're very much mistaken. No: and I'm not going to get out of my warm bed to let you in, either. No: nor Susan shan't sit up for you. No: nor you shan't have a latch-key. I'm not going to sleep with the door upon the latch, to be murdered before the morning.

"Faugh! Pah! Whewgh! That filthy tobacco-smoke! It's enough to kill any decent woman. You know I hate tobacco, and yet you will do it. *You don't smoke yourself*? What of that? If you go among people who *do* smoke, you're just as bad, or worse. You might as well smoke—indeed, better. Better smoke yourself than come home with other people's smoke all in your hair and whiskers.

"I never knew any good come to a man who went to a

7

tavern. Nice companions he picks up there! Yes; people who make it a boast to treat their wives like slaves, and ruin their families. There's that wretch, Harry Pretty-man. See what he's come to. He doesn't now get home till two in the morning; and then in what a state! He begins quarrelling with the door-mat, that his poor wife may be afraid to speak to him. A mean wretch! But don't you think I'll be like Mrs. Prettyman. No: I wouldn't put up with it from the best man that ever trod. You'll not make me afraid to speak to you, however you may swear at the door-mat. No, Mr. Caudle, that you won't.

"You don't intend to stay out till two in the morning?" How do you know what you'll do when you get among such people? Men can't answer for themselves when they get boozing one with another. They never think of their poor wives, who are grieving and wearing themselves out at home. A nice headache you'll have to-morrow morning— or rather *this* morning; for it must be past twelve. *You won't have a headache?* It's very well for you to say so, but I know you will; and then you may nurse yourself for me. Ha! that filthy tobacco again! No; I shall not go to sleep like a good soul. How's people to go to sleep when they're suffocated?

"Yes, Mr. Caudle, you'll be nice and ill in the morning! But don't you think I'm going to let you have your breakfast in bed, like Mrs. Prettyman. I'll not be such a fool. No; nor I won't have discredit brought upon the house by sending for soda-water early, for all the neighbourhood to say, 'Caudle was drunk last night.' No: I've some regard for the dear children, if you haven't. No: nor you shan't have broth for dinner. Not a neck of mutton crosses my threshold, I can tell you.

"You won't want soda, and you won't want broth?" All the

better. You wouldn't get 'em if you did, I can assure you.——Dear, dear, dear! That filthy tobacco! I'm sure it's enough to make me as bad as you are. Talking about getting divorced—I'm sure tobacco ought to be good grounds. How little does a woman think, when she marries, that she gives herself up to be poisoned! You men contrive to have it all of your own side, you do. Now if I was to go and leave you and the children, a pretty noise there'd be! You, however, can go and smoke no end of pipes and—*You didn't smoke?* It's all the same, Mr. Caudle, if you go among smoking people. Folks are known by their company. You'd better smoke yourself, than bring home the pipes of all the world.

"Yes, I see how it will be. Now you've once gone to a tavern, you'll always be going. You'll be coming home tipsy every night; and tumbling down and breaking your leg, and putting out your shoulder; and bringing all sorts

RETURNING FROM THE TAVERN.

of disgrace and expense upon us. And then you'll be getting into a street fight—oh! I know your temper too well to doubt it, Mr. Caudle—and be knocking down some of the police. And then I know what will follow. It *must* follow. Yes, you'll be sent for a month or six weeks to the treadmill. Pretty thing that, for a respectable tradesman, Mr. Caudle, to be put upon the treadmill with all sorts of thieves and vagabonds, and—there, again, that horrible tobacco!—and riffraff of every kind. I should like to know how your children are to hold up their heads, after their father has been upon the treadmill?——No; I *won't* go to sleep. And I'm not talking of what's impossible. I know it will all happen—every bit of it. If it wasn't for the dear children, you might be ruined and I wouldn't so much as speak about it, but—oh, dear, dear! at least you might go where they smoke *good* tobacco—but I can't forget that I'm their mother. At least, they shall have *one* parent.

"Taverns! Never did a man go to a tavern who didn't die a beggar. And how your pot-companions will laugh at you when they see your name in the Gazette! For it *must* happen. Your business is sure to fall off; for what respectable people will buy toys for their children of a drunkard? You're not a drunkard! No: but you will be—it's all the same.

"You've begun by staying out till midnight. By-and-by 'twill be all night. But don't you think, Mr. Caudle, you shall ever have a key. I know you. Yes; you'd do exactly like that Prettyman, and what did he do, only last Wednesday? Why, he let himself in about four in the morning, and brought home with him his pot-companion, Puffy. His dear wife woke at six, and saw Prettyman's dirty boots at her bed-side. And where was the wretch, her husband?

Why, he was drinking down stairs—swilling. Yes; worse than a midnight robber, he'd taken the keys out of his dear wife's pocket—ha! what that poor creature has to bear!— and had got at the brandy. A pretty thing for a wife to wake at six in the morning, and instead of her husband to see his dirty boots!

"But I'll not be made your victim, Mr. Caudle, not I. You shall never get at my keys, for they shall lie under my pillow—under my own head, Mr. Caudle.

"You'll be ruined, but if I can help it, you shall ruin nobody but yourself.

PRETTYMAN TAKING THE KEYS FROM HIS WIFE'S POCKET.

"Oh! that hor—hor—hor—i—ble tob—ac—co!"

To this lecture, Caudle affixes no comment. A certain proof, we think, that the man had nothing to say for himself.

Lecture III

Mr Caudle Joins a Club—
"The Skylarks"

"Well, if a woman hadn't better be in her grave than be married! That is, if she can't be married to a decent man. No; I don't care if you are tired, I *shan't* let you go to sleep. No, and I won't say what I have to say in the morning; I'll say it now. It's all very well for you to come home at what time you like—it's now half-past twelve—and expect I'm to hold my tongue, and let you go to sleep. What next, I wonder? A woman had better be sold for a slave at once.

"And so you've gone and joined a club? The Skylarks, indeed! A pretty skylark you'll make of yourself! But I won't stay and be ruined by you. No: I'm determined on that. I'll go and take the dear children, and you may get who you like to keep your house. That is, as long as you have a house to keep—and that won't be long, I know.

"How any decent man can go and spend his nights in a tavern?—oh, yes, Mr. Caudle; I dare say you *do* go for rational conversation. I should like to know how many of you would care for what you call rational conversation, if you had it without your filthy brandy-and-water; yes, and your more filthy tobacco-smoke. I'm sure the last time you came home, I had the

13

headache for a week. But I know who it is who's taking you to destruction. It's that brute, Prettyman. He has broken his own wife's heart, and now he wants to—but don't you think it, Mr. Caudle; I'll not have my peace of mind destroyed by the best man that ever trod. Oh, yes! I know you don't care so long as you can appear well to all the world—but the world little thinks how you behave to me. It shall know it, though—that I'm determined.

"How any man can leave his own happy fireside to go and sit, and smoke, and drink, and talk with people who wouldn't one of 'em lift a finger to save him from hanging—how any man can leave his wife—and a good wife, too, though I say it—for a parcel of pot-companions—oh, it's disgraceful, Mr. Caudle; it's un-feeling. No man who had the least love for his wife could do it.

"And I suppose this is to be the case every Saturday? But I know what I'll do. I know—it's no use, Mr. Caudle, your calling me a good creature: I'm not such a fool as to be coaxed in that way. No; if you want to go to sleep, you should come home in Christian time, not at half-past twelve. There was a time, when you were as regular at your fireside as the kettle. That was when you were a decent man, and didn't go amongst Heaven knows who, drinking and smoking, and making what you think your jokes. I never heard any good come to a man who cared about jokes. No respectable tradesman does. But I know what I'll do: I'll scare away your Skylarks. The house serves liquor after twelve of a Saturday; and if I don't write to the magistrates and have the licence taken away, I'm not lying in this bed this night. Yes, you may call me a foolish woman; but

HALF–PAST TWELVE AT THE CLUB.

no, Mr. Caudle, no; it's you who are the foolish man; or worse than a foolish man; you're a wicked one. If you were to die to-morrow—and people who go to public-houses do all they can to shorten their lives—I should like to know who would write upon your tombstone, 'A tender husband and an affectionate father?' *I*——I'd have no such falsehoods told of you, I can assure you.

"Going and spending your money, and—nonsense! don't tell me—no, if you were ten times to swear it, I wouldn't believe that you only spent eighteen-pence on a Saturday. You can't be all those hours, and only spend eighteen-pence. I know better. I'm not quite a fool, Mr. Caudle! A great deal you could have for eighteen-pence! And all the Club married men and fathers of families. The more shame for 'em! Skylarks, indeed! They should call themselves Vultures; for they can only do as

15

they do by eating up their innocent wives and children. Eighteen-pence a week! And if it was only that—do you know what fifty-two eighteen-pences come to in a year? Do you ever think of that, and see the gowns I wear? I'm sure I can't, out of the house-money, buy myself a pincushion; though I've wanted one these six months. No—not so much as a ball of cotton. But what do you care so you can get your brandy-and-water! There's the girls, too—the things they want! They're never dressed like other people's children. But it's all the same to their father. Oh yes! So he can go with his Skylarks they may wear sackcloth for pinafores, and packthread for garters.

"You'd better not let that Mr. Prettyman come here, that's all; or, rather, you'd better bring him once. Yes, I should like to see him. He wouldn't forget it. A man who, I may say, lives and moves only in a spittoon. A man who has a pipe in his mouth as constant as his front teeth. A sort of tavern king, with a lot of fools, like you, to laugh at what he thinks his jokes, and give him consequence. No, Mr. Caudle, no; it's no use your telling me to go to sleep, for I won't. Go to sleep, indeed! I'm sure it's almost time to get up. I hardly know what's the use of coming to bed at all now.

"The Skylarks, indeed! I suppose you'll be buying a 'Little Warbler' and at your time of life, be trying to sing. The peacocks will sing next. A pretty name you'll get in the neighbourhood; and, in a very little time, a nice face you'll have. Your nose is getting redder already: and you've just one of the noses that liquor always flies to. *You don't see it's red?* No—I dare say not—but *I* see it; *I* see a great many things you don't. And so you'll go on. In a little time, with your brandy-

and-water—don't tell me that you only take two small glasses: I know what men's two small glasses are; in a little time you'll have a face all over as if it was made of red currant jam. And I should like to know who's to endure you then? I won't, and so don't think it. Don't come to me.

"Nice habits men learn at clubs! There's Joskins: he was a decent creature once, and now I'm told he has more than once boxed his wife's ears. He's a Skylark too. And I suppose, some day, you'll be trying to box *my* ears? Don't attempt it, Mr. Caudle; I say don't attempt it. Yes—it's all very well for you to say you don't mean it—but I only say again, don't attempt it. You'd rue it till the day of your death, Mr. Caudle.

"Going and sitting for four hours at a tavern! What men, unless they had their wives with them, can find to talk about, I can't think. No good, of course.

"Eighteen-pence a week—and drinking brandy-and-water, enough to swim a boat! And smoking like the funnel of a steamship! And I can't afford myself so much as a piece of tape! It's brutal, Mr. Caudle. It's ve-ve-ve—ry bru—tal."

"And here," says Caudle—"Here, thank Heaven! at last she fell asleep."

Lecture IV

Mr. Caudle Has Been Called from his Bed to Bail Mr. Prettyman from the Watch-House

"Yes, Mr. Caudle, I knew it would come to this. I said it would, when you joined those precious Skylarks. People being called out of their beds at all hours of the night, to bail a set of fellows who are never so happy as when they're leading sober men to destruction. I should like to know what the neighbours will think of you, with people from the police knocking at the door at two in the morning? Don't tell me that the man has been ill-used: he's not the man to be ill-used. And you must go and bail him! I know the end of that: he'll run away, and you'll have to pay the money. I should like to know what's the use of my working and slaving to save a farthing, when you throw away pounds upon your precious Skylarks. A pretty cold you'll have to-morrow morning, being called out of your warm bed this weather; but don't you think I'll nurse you—not I! not a drop of gruel do you get from me.

"I'm sure you've plenty of ways of spending your money—not throwing it away upon a set of dissolute peace-breakers. It's all very well for you to say you haven't thrown away your money, but you will. He'll be certain to run off; it isn't likely he'll go upon his trial, and you'll be fixed with the bail. Don't tell me there's

MR. CAUDLE IS CALLED UP AT TWO IN THE MORNING.

no trial in the matter, because I know there is; it's for something more than quarrelling with the policeman that he was locked up. People ar'n't locked up for that. No, it's for robbery, or something worse, perhaps.

"And as you've bailed him, people will think you are as bad as he is. Don't tell me you couldn't help bailing him; you should have shown yourself a respectable man, and have let him been sent to prison.

"Now people know you're the friend of drunken and disorderly persons, you'll never have a night's sleep in

MR. CAUDLE AND THE POLICE.

your bed. Not that it would matter what fell upon you, if it wasn't your poor wife who suffered. Of course all the business will be in the newspapers, and your name with it. I shouldn't wonder, too, if they give your picture as they do the other folks of the Old Bailey. A pretty thing that, to go down to your children. I'm sure it will be enough to make them change their name. No, I shall not go to sleep; it's all very well for you to say, go to sleep, after such a disturbance. But I shall not go to sleep, Mr. Caudle; certainly not."

"Her will, I have no doubt," says Caudle, "was strong; but nature was stronger, and she *did* sleep; this night inflicting upon me a remarkably short lecture."

Lecture V

Mr. Caudle Has Remained Down Stairs Till Past One, with a Friend

"Pretty time of night to come to bed, Mr. Caudle. Ugh! As cold, too, as any ice. Enough to give any woman her death, I'm sure. What! *I shouldn't have locked up the coals?* If I hadn't, I've no doubt the fellow would have stayed all night. It's all very well for you, Mr. Caudle, to bring people home—but I wish you'd think first what's for supper. That beautiful leg of pork would have served for our dinner to-morrow—and now it's gone. *I* can't keep the house upon the money, and I won't pretend to do it, if you bring a mob of people every night to clear out the cupboard.

"I wonder who'll be so ready to give you a supper when you want one: for want one you will, unless you change your plans. Don't tell me! I know I'm right. You'll first be eaten up, and then you'll be laughed at. I know the world. No, indeed, Mr. Caudle, I don't think ill of everybody; don't say that. But I can't see a leg of pork eaten up in that way, without asking myself what it's all to end in if such things go on? And then he must have pickles, too! Couldn't be content with my cabbage —no, Mr. Caudle, I won't let you go to sleep. It's very well for you to say let you go to sleep, after you've kept me awake till this time. *Why did I keep awake?* How do

23

you suppose I could go to sleep, when I knew that man was below drinking up your substance in brandy-and-water? for he couldn't be content upon decent, wholesome gin. Upon my word, you ought to be a rich man, Mr. Caudle. You have such very fine friends. I wonder who gives you brandy when you go out!

"No, indeed, he couldn't be content with my pickled cabbage—and I should like to know who makes better—but he must have walnuts. And you, too, like a fool—now, don't you think to stop me, Mr. Caudle; a poor woman may be trampled to death, and never say a word—you, too, like a fool—I wonder who'd do it for you—to insist upon the girl going out for pickled walnuts. And in such a night too! With snow upon the ground. Yes: you're a man of fine feelings, you are, Mr. Caudle; but the world doesn't know you as I know you—fine feelings, indeed! to send the poor girl out, when I told you and told your friend, too—a pretty brute he is, I'm sure—that the poor girl had got a cold and I dare say chilblains on her toes. But I know what will be the end of that; she'll be laid up, and we shall have a nice doctor's bill. And you'll pay it, I can tell you—for *I* won't.

"*You wish you were out of the world?* Oh! yes, that's all very easy. I'm sure *I* might wish it. Don't swear in that dreadful way! Ar'n't you afraid that the bed will open and swallow you? And don't swing about in that way. *That* will do no good. *That* won't bring back the leg of pork, and the brandy you've poured down both of your throats. Oh, I know it. I'm sure of it. I only recollected it when I'd got into bed—and if it hadn't been so cold, you'd have seen me down stairs again, I can tell you—I recollected it, and a pretty two hours I've passed—that

MR. CAUDLE HAS SENT THE GIRL OUT.

I left the key in the cupboard—and I know it—I could see by the manner of you, when you came into the room—I know you've got at the other bottle. However, there's one comfort: you told me to send for the best brandy—the very best—for your other friend, who called last Wednesday. Ha! ha! It was British—the cheapest British—and nice and ill I hope the pair of you will be to-morrow.

"There's only the bare bone of the leg of pork; but you'll get nothing else for dinner, I can tell you. It's a

25

dreadful thing that the poor children should go without—but, if they have such a father, they, poor things, must suffer for it.

"Nearly a whole leg of pork and a pint of brandy! A pint of brandy and a leg of pork."

Lecture VI

Mr. Caudle Has Lent an Acquaintance the Family Umbrella

"That's the third umbrella gone since Christmas. *What were you to do?* Why let him go home in the rain, to be sure. I'm very certain there was nothing about *him* that could spoil. Take cold, indeed! He doesn't look like one of the sort to take cold. Besides, he'd have better taken cold than take our only umbrella. Do you hear the rain, Mr. Caudle? I say, do you hear the rain? And as I'm alive, if it isn't St. Swithin's day! Do you hear it against the windows? Nonsense; you don't impose upon me. You can't be asleep with such a shower as that! Do you hear it, I say? Oh, you *do* hear it! Well, that's a pretty flood, I think, to last for six weeks; and no stirring all the time out of the house. Pooh! don't think me a fool, Mr. Caudle. Don't insult me. *He* return the umbrella! Anybody would think you were born yesterday. As if anybody ever *did* return an umbrella! There—do you hear it? Worse and worse? Cats and dogs, and for six weeks—always six weeks. And no umbrella!

"I should like to know how the children are to go to school to-morrow? They shan't go through such weather, I'm determined. No: they shall stop at home and never learn anything—the blessed creatures!— sooner than go and get wet. And when they grow up, I

27

MRS. CAUDLE OBJECTS TO LENDING THE UMBRELLA.

wonder who they'll have to thank for knowing nothing—who, indeed, but their father? People who can't feel for their own children ought never to be fathers.

"But I know why you lent the umbrella. Oh, yes; I know very well. I was going out to tea at dear mother's to-morrow—you knew that; and you did it on purpose. Don't tell me; you hate me to go there, and take every mean advantage to hinder me. But don't you think it, Mr. Caudle. No, sir; if it comes down in buckets-full,

I'll go all the more. No: and I won't have a cab. Where do you think the money's to come from? You've got nice high notions at that club of yours. A cab, indeed! Cost me sixteen-pence at least—sixteen-pence! two-and-eightpence! for there's back again. Cabs, indeed! I should like to know who's to pay for 'em; *I* can't pay for 'em, and I'm sure you can't, if you go on as you do; throwing away your property, and beggaring your children—buying umbrellas!

"Do you hear the rain, Mr. Caudle? I say, do you hear it? But I don't care—I'll go to mother's to-morrow: I will; and what's more, I'll walk every step of the way—and you know that will give me my death. Don't call me a foolish woman, it's you that's the foolish man. You know I can't wear clogs; and with no umbrella, the wet's sure to give me a cold—it always does. But what do you

MRS. CAUDLE "WON'T HAVE A CAB."

care for that! Nothing at all. I may be laid up for what you care, as I dare say I shall—and a pretty doctor's bill there'll be. I hope there will! It will teach you to lend your umbrellas again. I shouldn't wonder if I caught my death; yes: and that's what you lent the umbrella for. Of course!

"Nice clothes, I shall get too, trapesing through weather like this. My gown and bonnet will be spoilt quite. *Needn't I wear 'em then?* Indeed, Mr. Caudle, I *shall* wear 'em. No, sir, I'm not going out a dowdy to please you or anybody else. Gracious knows! It isn't often that I step over the threshold; indeed, I might as well be a slave at once—better, I should say. But when I do go out, Mr. Caudle, I choose to go like a lady. Oh! that rain—if it isn't enough to break in the windows.

"Ugh! I do look forward with dread for to-morrow! How I am to go to mother's I'm sure I can't tell. But if I die, I'll do it. No, sir; I won't borrow an umbrella. No; and you shan't buy one. Now, Mr. Caudle, only listen to this: if you bring home another umbrella, I'll throw it in the street. I'll have my own umbrella, or none at all.

"Ha! and it was only last week I had a new nozzle put to that umbrella. I'm sure, if I'd have known as much as I do now, it might have gone without one for me. Paying for new nozzles, for other people to laugh at you. Oh, it's all very well for you—you can go to sleep. You've no thought of your poor patient wife, and your own dear children. You think of nothing but lending umbrellas.

"Men, indeed!—call themselves lords of the creation! —pretty lords, when they can't even take care of an umbrella!

"I know that walk to-morrow will be the death of me. But that's what you want—then you may go to your club, and do as you like—and then, nicely my poor dear children will be used—but then, sir, then you'll be happy. Oh, don't tell me! I know you will. Else you'd never have lent the umbrella!

"You have to go on Thursday about that summons; and, of course, you can't go. No, indeed, you *don't* go without the umbrella. You may lose the debt for what I care—it won't be so much as spoiling your clothes—better lose it: people deserve to lose debts who lend umbrellas!

"And I should like to know how I'm to go to mother's without the umbrella? Oh, don't tell me that I said I *would* go—that's nothing to do with it; nothing at all. She'll think I'm neglecting her, and the little money we were to have, we shan't have at all—because we've no umbrella.

"The children, too! Dear things! They'll be sopping wet: for they shan't stop at home—they shan't lose their learning; it's all their father will leave 'em, I'm sure. But *they* shall go to school. Don't tell me I said they shouldn't: you are so aggravating, Caudle; you'd spoil the temper of an angel. They *shall* go to school; mark that. And if they get their deaths of cold, it's not my fault—I didn't lend the umbrella."

"At length," writes Caudle, "I fell asleep; and dreamt that the sky was turned into green calico, with whale-bone ribs; that, in fact, the whole world turned round under a tremendous umbrella!"

Lecture VII

Mr. Caudle Has Ventured a Remonstrance on his Day's Dinner: Cold Mutton, and No Pudding. Mrs. Caudle Defends the Cold Shoulder

"I'm sure! Well! I wonder what it will be next? There's nothing proper, now—nothing at all. Better get somebody else to keep the house, I think. I can't do it now, it seems; I'm only in the way here: I'd better take the children, and go.

"What am I grumbling about now? It's very well for you to ask that! I'm sure I'd better be out of the world than—there now, Mr. Caudle; there you are again! I *shall* speak, sir. It isn't often I open my mouth, Heaven knows! But you like to hear nobody talk but yourself. You ought to have married a Negro slave, and not any respectable woman.

"You're to go about the house looking like thunder all the day, and I'm not to say a word. Where do you think pudding's to come from every day? You show a nice example to your children, you do; complaining, and turning your nose up at a sweet piece of cold mutton, because there's no pudding! You go a nice way to make 'em extravagant—teach 'em nice lessons to begin the world with. Do you know what puddings cost; or do you think they fly in at the window?

"You hate cold mutton. The more shame for you, Mr. Caudle. I'm sure you've the stomach of a lord, you

MR. CAUDLE DINES AT HOME. COLD MUTTON!

have. No, sir; I didn't choose to hash the mutton. It's very easy for you to say hash it; but *I* know what a joint loses in hashing; it's a day's dinner the less, if it's a bit. Yes, I dare say; other people may have puddings with cold mutton. No doubt of it; and other people become bankrupts. But if ever you get into the Gazette, it shan't be *my* fault—no; I'll do my duty as a wife to you, Mr. Caudle: you shall never have it to say that it was *my* housekeeping that brought you to beggary. No; you may sulk at the cold meat—ha! I hope you'll never live to want such a piece of cold mutton as we had to-day! and you may threaten to go to a tavern to dine; but, with our present means, not a crumb of pudding do you get from me. You shall have nothing but the cold joint—nothing as I'm a Christian sinner.

"Yes; there you are, throwing those fowls in my face again! I know you once brought home a pair of fowls; I know it: and wer'n't you mean enough to want to stop 'em out of my week's money? Oh, the selfishness—the shabbiness of men! They can go out and throw away pounds upon pounds with a pack of people who laugh at 'em afterwards; but if it's anything wanted for their own homes, their poor wives may hunt for it. I wonder you don't blush to name those fowls again! I wouldn't be so little for the world, Mr. Caudle.

"What are you going to do? *Going to get up?* Don't make yourself ridiculous, Mr. Caudle; I can't say a word to you like any other wife, but you must threaten to get up. *Do* be ashamed of yourself.

"Puddings, indeed! Do you think I'm made of puddings? Didn't you have some boiled rice three weeks ago? Besides, is this the time of the year for puddings? It's all very well if I had money enough allowed me like any other wife to keep the house with: then, indeed, I might have preserves like any other woman; now, it's impossible; and it's cruel—yes, Mr. Caudle, cruel—of you to expect it.

"*Apples arn't so dear, are they?* I know what apples are, Mr. Caudle, without your telling me. But I suppose you want something more than apples for dumplings? I suppose sugar costs something, doesn't it? And that's how it is. That's how one expense brings on another, and that's how people go to ruin.

"*Pancakes?* What's the use of your lying muttering there about pancakes? Don't you always have 'em once a year—every Shrove Tuesday? And what would any moderate, decent man want more?

"Pancakes, indeed! Pray, Mr. Caudle—no, it's no use your saying fine words to me to let you go to sleep; I shan't!—pray do you know the price of eggs just now? There's not an egg you can trust to under seven and eight a shilling; well, you've only just to reckon up how many eggs—don't lie swearing there at the eggs, in that manner, Mr. Caudle; unless you expect the bed to let you fall through. You call yourself a respectable trades-man, I suppose? Ha! I only wish people knew you as well as I do! Swearing at eggs, indeed! But I'm tired of this usage, Mr. Caudle; quite tired of it; and I don't care how soon it's ended!

"I'm sure I do nothing but work and labour, and think how to make the most of everything: and this is how I'm rewarded. I should like to see anybody whose joints go further than mine. But if I was to throw away your money into the street, or lay it out in fine feathers on myself, I should be better thought of. The woman who studies her husband and her family is always made a drudge of. It's your fine fal-lal wives who've the best time of it.

"What's the use of your lying groaning there in that manner? That won't make me hold my tongue, I can tell you. You think to have it all your own way—but you won't, Mr. Caudle! You can insult my dinner; look like a demon, I may say, at a wholesome piece of cold mutton—ha! the thousands of far better creatures than you are who'd been thankful for that mutton!—and I'm never to speak! But you're mistaken—I will! Your usage of me, Mr. Caudle, is infamous—unworthy of a man. I only wish people knew you for what you are; but I've told you again and again they shall some day.

"Puddings! And now I suppose I shall hear of nothing but puddings! Yes, and I know what it would end in. First, you'd have a pudding every day!—oh, I know your extravagance—then you'd go for fish—then I shouldn't wonder if you'd have soup; turtle, no doubt: then you'd go for a dessert; and—oh! I see it all as plain as the quilt before me—but no, not while I'm alive! What your second wife may do, I don't know; perhaps *she'll* be a fine lady; but you shan't be ruined by me, Mr. Caudle; that I'm determined. Puddings, indeed! Pu-dding-s! Pudd—"

"Exhausted nature," says Caudle, "could hold out no longer. She went to sleep."

Lecture VIII

Caudle Has Been Made a Mason. Mrs. Caudle Indignant and Curious

"Now, Mr. Caudle—Mr. Caudle, I say: oh! you can't be asleep already, I know—now, what I mean to say is this; there's no use, none at all, in our having any disturbance about the matter; but at last my mind's made up, Mr. Caudle; I shall leave you. Either I know all you've been doing to-night, or to-morrow morning I quit the house. No, no; there's an end of the marriage-state, I think— an end of all confidence between man and wife—if a husband's to have secrets and keep 'em all to himself. Pretty secrets they must be, when his own wife can't know 'em! Not fit for any decent person to know, I'm sure, if that's the case. Now, Caudle, don't let us quarrel; there's a good soul, tell me what's it all about? A pack of nonsense, I dare say; still—not that I care much about it—still, I *should* like to know. There's a dear. Eh? Oh, don't tell me there's nothing in it: I know better. I'm not a fool, Mr. Caudle; I know there's a good deal in it. Now, Caudle; just tell me a little bit of it. I'm sure I'd tell you anything. You know I would. Well?

"Caudle, you're enough to vex a saint! Now don't you think you're going to sleep; because you're not. Do you suppose I'd ever suffered you to go and be made a mason, if I didn't suppose I was to know the secret, too?

39

Not that it's anything to know, I dare say; and that's why I'm determined to know it.

"But I know what it is; oh yes, there can be no doubt. The secret is, to ill-use poor women; to tyrannise over 'em; to make 'em your slaves; especially your wives. It must be something of the sort, or you wouldn't be ashamed to have it known. What's right and proper never need be done in secret. It's an insult to a woman for a man to be a free-mason, and let his wife know nothing of it. But, poor soul! she's sure to know it somehow—for nice husbands they all make. Yes, yes; a part of the secret is to think better of all the world than their own wives and families. I'm sure men have quite enough to care for—that is, if they act properly—to care for them they have at home. They can't have much care to spare for the world besides.

"And I suppose they call you *Brother* Caudle? A pretty brother, indeed! Going and dressing yourself up in an apron like a turnpike man—for that's what you look like.

"WHAT'S THE APRON FOR, MR. CAUDLE?"

And I should like to know what the apron's for? There must be something in it not very respectable, I'm sure. Well, I only wish I was Queen for a day or two. I'd put an end to free-masonry, and all such trumpery, I know.

"Now, come, Caudle; don't let's quarrel. Eh! You're not in pain, dear? What's it all about? What are you lying laughing there at? But I'm a fool to trouble my head about you.

"And you're not going to let me know the secret, eh? You mean to say—you're not? Now, Caudle, you know it's a hard matter to put me in a passion—not that I care about the secret itself: no, I wouldn't give a button to know it, for it's all nonsense, I'm sure. It isn't the secret I care about: it's the slight, Mr. Caudle; it's the studied insult that a man pays to his wife, when he thinks of going through the world keeping something to himself which he won't let her know. Man and wife one, indeed! I should like to know how that can be when a man's a mason—when he keeps a secret that sets him and his wife apart? Ha, you men make the laws, and so you take good care to have all the best of 'em to yourselves; otherwise a woman ought to be allowed a divorce when a man becomes a mason; when he's got a sort of corner-cupboard in his heart—a secret place in his mind—that his poor wife isn't allowed to rummage!

"Caudle, you shan't close your eyes for a week—no, you shan't—unless you tell me some of it. Come, there's a good creature; there's a love. I'm sure, Caudle, I wouldn't refuse you anything—and you know it, or ought to know it by this time. I only wish I had a secret! To whom should I think of confiding it, but to my dear husband? I should be miserable to keep it to myself, and you know it. Now, Caudle?

"LODGE, INDEED! NICE GOINGS ON, I DARE SAY."

"Was there ever such a man? A man, indeed! A brute!—yes, Mr. Caudle, an unfeeling brutal creature, when you might oblige me, and you won't. I'm sure I don't object to your being a mason; not at all, Caudle; I dare say it's a very good thing; I dare say it is—it's only your making a secret of it that vexes me. But you'll tell me—you'll tell your own Margaret? You won't! You're a wretch, Mr. Caudle.

"But I know why: oh, yes, I can tell. The fact is, you're ashamed to let me know what a fool they've been making of you. That's it. You, at your time of life—the

42

father of a family! I should be ashamed of myself, Caudle.

"And I suppose you'll be going to what you call your Lodge every night, now? Lodge, indeed! Pretty place it must be, where they don't admit women. Nice goings on, I dare say. Then you call one another brethren. Brethren! I'm sure you'd relations enough, you didn't want any more.

"But I know what all this masonry's about. It's only an excuse to get away from your wives and families, that you may feast and drink together, that's all. That's the secret. And to abuse women—as if they were inferior animals, and not to be trusted. That's the secret; and nothing else.

"Now, Caudle, don't let us quarrel. Yes, I know you're in pain. Still Caudle, my love; Caudle! Dearest, I say! Caudle!"

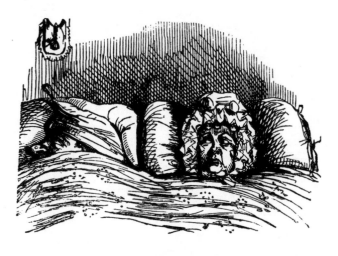

MR. AND MRS. CAUDLE.

"I recollect nothing more," says Caudle, "for I had eaten a hearty supper, and somehow became oblivious."

Lecture IX

Mr. Caudle Has Been to Greenwich Fair

"So, Mr. Caudle: I hope you enjoyed yourself at Greenwich. *How do I know you've been at Greenwich?* I know it very well, sir; know all about it: know more than you think I know. I thought there was something in the wind. Yes, I was sure of it, when you went out of the house, to-day. I knew it by the looks of you, though I didn't say anything. Upon my word! And you call yourself a respectable man, and the father of a family! Going to a fair among all sorts of people—at your time of life. Yes; and never think of taking your wife with you. Oh no! you can go and enjoy yourself out, with *I* don't know who: go out, and make yourself very pleasant, I dare say. Don't tell me; I hear what a nice companion Mr. Caudle is: what a good-tempered person. Ha! I only wish people could see you at home, that's all. But so it is with men. They can keep all their good temper for out-of-doors—their wives never see any of it. Oh dear! I'm sure I don't know who'd be a poor woman!

"Now, Caudle, I'm not in an ill temper; not at all. I know I used to be a fool when we were first married: I used to worry and fret myself to death when you went out; but I've got over that. I wouldn't put myself out of

45

MR. CAULDE AT THE FAIR.

the way now for the best man that ever trod. For what thanks does a poor woman get? None at all. No: it's those who don't care for their families, who are the best thought of. I only wish I could bring myself not to care for mine.

"And why couldn't you say, like a man, you were going to Greenwich Fair when you went out? It's no use your saying that, Mr. Caudle: don't tell me that you didn't think of going; you'd made your mind up to it, and you know it. Pretty games you've had, no doubt! I should like to have been behind you, that's all. A man at your time of life!

"And I, of course, I never want to go out. Oh no! I may stay at home with the cat. You couldn't think of taking your wife and children, like any other decent man, to a fair. Oh no; you never care to be seen with us.

I'm sure many people don't know you're married at all: how can they? Your wife's never seen with you. Oh no; anybody but those belonging to you!

"Greenwich Fair, indeed! Yes—and of course you went up and down the hill, running and racing with nobody knows who. Don't tell me; I know what you are when you're out. You don't suppose, Mr. Caudle, I've forgotten that pink bonnet, do you? No: I won't hold my tongue, and I'm not a foolish woman. It's no matter, sir, if the pink bonnet was fifty years ago—it's all the same for that. No: and if I live for fifty years to come, I never will leave off talking of it. You ought to be ashamed of yourself, Mr. Caudle. Ha! few wives would have been what I've been to you. I only wish my time was to come over again, that's all; I wouldn't be the fool I have been.

"Going to a fair! and I suppose you had your fortune told by the gipsies! You needn't have wasted your money. I'm sure I can tell you your fortune if you go on as you do. Yes, the gaol will be your fortune, Mr. Caudle. And it would be no matter—none at all—if your wife and children didn't suffer with you.

"And then you must go riding upon donkeys.— *You didn't go riding upon donkeys?* Yes; it's very well for you to say so: but I dare say you did. I tell you, Caudle, I know what you are when you're out. I wouldn't trust any of you—you, especially, Caudle.

"Then you must go in the thick of the fair, and have the girls scratching your coat with rattles! *You couldn't help it, if they did scratch your coat?* Don't tell me; people don't scratch coats unless they're encouraged to do it. And you must go in a swing, too. *You didn't go in a swing?* Well, if you didn't, it was no fault of yours; you

47

wish'd to go, I've no doubt.

"And then you must go into the shows? There—you don't deny that. You did go into a show. *What of it, Mr. Caudle?*—A good deal of it, sir. Nice crowding and squeezing in those shows, I know. Pretty places! And you a married man and the father of a family. No, I won't hold my tongue. It's very well for you to threaten to get up. You're to go to Greenwich Fair, and race up and down the hill, and play at kiss in the ring. Pah! it's disgusting, Mr. Caudle. Oh, I dare say you *did* play at it; if you didn't, you'd have liked, and that's just as bad—and you can go into swings, and shows, and round-abouts. If I was you, I should hide my head under the clothes, and be ashamed of myself.

"And what is most selfish—most mean of you, Caudle—you can go and enjoy yourself, and never so much as bring home for the poor children a gingerbread nut. Don't tell me that your pocket was picked of a pound of nuts! Nice company you must have been in to have your pocket picked.

"But I dare say I shall hear all about it to-morrow. I've no doubt, sir, you were dancing at the Crown-and-Anchor. I should like to have seen you. No: I'm not making myself ridiculous. It's you that's making yourself ridiculous, and everybody that knows you says so. Everybody knows what I have to put up with from you.

"Going to a fair, indeed! At your time——'

"Here," says Caudle, "I dozed off, hearing confusedly the words—hill—gipsies—rattles—round-abouts—swings—pink bonnet—nuts."

Lecture X

On Mr. Caudle's Shirt-Buttons

"Well, Mr. Caudle, I hope you're in a little better temper than you were this morning? There—you needn't begin to whistle: people don't come to bed to whistle. But it's like you. I can't speak that you don't try to insult me. Once, I used to say you were the best creature living: now, you get quite a fiend. *Do let you rest?* No, I won't let you rest. It's the only time I have to talk to you, and you *shall* hear me. I'm put upon all day long: it's very hard if I can't speak a word at night: besides it isn't often I open my mouth, goodness knows!

"Because *once* in your lifetime your shirt wanted a button, you must almost swear the roof off the house! *You didn't swear?* Ha, Mr. Caudle! you don't know what you do when you're in a passion. *You were not in a passion?* Wer'n't you? Well, then, I don't know what a passion is—and I think I ought by this time; I've lived long enough with you, Mr. Caudle, to know that.

"It's a pity you haven't something worse to complain of than a button off your shirt. If you'd *some* wives, you would, I know. I'm sure I'm never without a needle-and-thread in my hand. What with you and the children, I'm made a perfect slave of. And what's my thanks? Why, if once in your life a button's off

49

MR. CAUDLE FINDS A BUTTON OFF HIS SHIRT.

your shirt—what do you cry '*oh*' at?—I say once, Mr. Caudle; or twice, or three times, at most. I'm sure, Caudle, no man's buttons in the world are better looked after than yours. I only wish I had kept the shirts you had when you were first married! I should like to know where were your buttons then?

"Yes. It *is* worth talking of! But that's how you always try to put me down. You fly into a rage, and then if I only try to speak you won't hear me. That's how you men always will have all the talk to yourselves: a poor woman isn't allowed to get a word in.

"A nice notion you have of a wife, to suppose she's nothing to think of but her husband's buttons. A pretty notion, indeed, you have of marriage. Ha! if poor women only knew what they had to go through! What with buttons, and one thing and another! They'd never tie themselves up—no, not to the best man in the world, I'm sure. *What would they do, Mr. Caudle?* Why, do much better without you, I'm certain.

"And it's my belief, after all, that the button wasn't off the shirt; it's my belief that you pulled it off, that you might have something to talk about. Oh! you're aggravating enough, when you like, for anything! All I know is, it's very odd that the button should be off the shirt; for I'm sure no woman's a greater slave to her husband's buttons than I am. I only say, it's very odd.

"However, there's one comfort; it can't last long. I'm worn to death with your temper, and shan't trouble you a great while. Ha, you may laugh! And I dare say you would laugh! I've no doubt of it! That's your love— that's your feeling! I know that I'm sinking every day, though I say nothing about it. And when I'm gone, we shall see how your second wife will look after your buttons. You'll find out the difference, then. Yes, Caudle, you'll think of me then: for then, I hope, you'll never have a blessed button to your back.

"No, I'm not a vindictive woman, Mr. Caudle; nobody ever called me that, but you. What do you say? *Nobody ever knew so much of me?* That's nothing at all to do with it. Ha! I wouldn't have your aggravating temper, Caudle, for mines of gold. It's a good thing I'm not as worrying as you are—or a nice house there'd be between us. I only wish you'd had a wife that *would* have talked to you! Then you'd have known the difference. But you impose upon me, because, like a poor fool, I say nothing. I should be ashamed of myself, Caudle.

"And a pretty example you set as a father! You'll make your boys as bad as yourself. Talking as you did all breakfast-time about your buttons! And of a Sunday morning too! And you call yourself a Christian; I should like to know what your boys will say of you when they grow up? And all about a paltry button off one of your wristbands? A decent man wouldn't have mentioned it. *Why won't I hold my tongue?* Because I *won't* hold my tongue. I'm to have my peace of mind destroyed—I'm to be worried into my grave for a miserable shirt-button, and I'm to hold my tongue! Oh! but that's just like you men!

"But I know what I'll do for the future. Every button you have may drop off, and I won't so much as put a thread to 'em. And I should like to know what you'll do then? Oh, you must get somebody else to sew 'em, must you? That's a pretty threat for a husband to hold out to a wife! And to such a wife as I've been, too; such a Negro slave to your buttons, as I may say! Somebody else to sew 'em, eh? No, Caudle, no: not while I'm alive! When I'm dead—and with what I have to bear there's no knowing how soon that may be—when I'm dead, I say—oh! what a brute you must be to snore so!

"*You're not snoring?* Ha! that's what you always say; but that's nothing to do with it. You must get somebody else to sew 'em, must you? Ha! I shouldn't wonder. Oh no! I should be surprised at nothing, now. Nothing at all! It's what people have always told me it would come to—and now, the buttons have opened my eyes! But the whole world shall know of your cruelty, Mr. Caudle. After the wife I've been to you. Somebody else, indeed, to sew your buttons! I'm no longer to be mistress in my own house! Ha, Caudle! I wouldn't have upon my conscience what you have, for the world! I wouldn't treat anybody as you treat—no, I'm not mad! It's you, Mr. Caudle, who are mad, or bad—and that's worse! I can't even so much as speak of a shirt-button, but that I'm threatened to be made nobody of in my own house! Caudle, you've a heart like a hearth-stone, you have! To threaten me, and only because a button—a button——"

"I was conscious of no more than this," says Caudle: "for here nature relieved me with a sweet, deep sleep."

Lecture XI

Mrs. Caudle Suggests that her Dear Mother Should "Come and Live with Them"

"Is your cold better to-night, Caudle? Yes; I thought it was. 'Twill be quite well to-morrow, I dare say. There's a love! You don't take care enough of yourself, Caudle, you don't. And you ought, I'm sure; if only for my sake. For whatever I should do, if anything was to happen to you—but I won't think of it; no I can't bear to think of *that*. Still, you ought to take care of yourself; for you know you're not strong, Caudle; you know you're not.

"Wasn't dear mother so happy with us to-night? Now, you needn't go to sleep so suddenly. I say, wasn't she so happy. *You don't know*? How can you say you don't know? You must have seen it. But she always is happier here than anywhere else. Ha! what a temper that dear soul has! I call it a temper of satin; it is so smooth, so easy, and so soft. Nothing puts her out of the way. And then, if you only knew how she takes your part, Caudle! I'm sure, if you had been her own son ten times over, she couldn't be fonder of you. Don't you think so, Caudle! Eh, love? Now, do answer. *How can you tell*? Nonsense, Caudle; you must have seen it. I'm sure, nothing delights the dear soul so much as when she's thinking how to please you.

"Don't you remember Thursday night, the stewed

55

oysters when you came home? That was all dear mother's doings! 'Margaret,' says she to me, 'it's a cold night; and don't you think dear Mr. Caudle would like something nice before he goes to bed?' And that, Caudle, is how the oysters came about. Now, don't sleep, Caudle: do listen to me, for five minutes; 'tisn't often I speak, goodness knows.

"And then what a fuss she makes when you're out, if your slippers ar'n't put to the fire for you. *She's very good?* Yes—I know she is, Caudle. And hasn't she been six months—though I promised her not to tell you—six months, working a watch-pocket for you! And with her eyes, dear soul—and at *her* time of life!

"And then what a cook she is! I'm sure, the dishes she'll make out of next to nothing! I try hard enough to follow her; but, I'm not ashamed to own it, Caudle, she quite beats me. Ha! the many nice little things she'd simmer up for you—and I can't do it; the children, you know it, Caudle, take so much of my time. I can't do it, love: and I often reproach myself that I can't. Now, you shan't go to sleep, Caudle, at least, not for five minutes. You must hear me.

"I've been thinking, dearest—ha! that nasty cough, love!—I've been thinking, darling, if we could only persuade dear mother to come and live with us. Now, Caudle, you can't be asleep; it's impossible—you were coughing only this minute—yes, to live with us. What a treasure we should have in her! Then, Caudle, you never need go to bed without something nice and hot. And you want it, Caudle. *You don't want it?* Nonsense, you do; for you're not strong, Caudle; you know you're not.

"I'm sure, the money she'd save us in housekeeping. Ha! what an eye she has a for a joint! the butcher doesn't walk that could deceive dear mother. And then, again, for poultry; what a finger and thumb she has for a chicken! I never could market like her: it's a gift—quite a gift.

"And then you recollect her marrow-puddings? *You don't recollect 'em*? Oh, fie! Caudle, how often have you flung her marrow-puddings in my face, wanting to know why I couldn't make 'em? And I wouldn't pretend to do it after dear mother; I should think it presumption. Now, love, if she was only living with us— come, you're not asleep, Caudle—if she was only living with us, you could have marrow-puddings every day. Now, don't fling yourself about and begin to swear at marrow-puddings; you know you like 'em, dear.

"What a hand, too, dear mother has for a pie-crust. But it's born with some people. What do you say? *Why wasn't it born with me*? Now, Caudle, that's cruel— unfeeling of you; I wouldn't have uttered such a reproach to you for the whole world. Consider, dear; people can't be born as they like.

"How often, too, have you wanted to brew at home! And I never could learn anything about brewing. But, ha! what ale dear mother makes! *You never tasted it*? No, I know that. But I recollect the ale we used to have at home: and father never would drink wine after it. The best sherry was nothing like it. *You dare say not*? No; it wasn't indeed, Caudle. Then, if dear mother was only with us, what money we should save in beer! And then you might always have your own nice, pure, good, wholesome ale, Caudle: and what good it would do you! For you're not strong, Caudle.

"And then dear mother's jams and preserves, love! I own it, Caudle; it has often gone to my heart that with cold meat you hav'n't always had a pudding. Now, if mother was with us, in the matter of fruit puddings, she'd make it summer all the year round. But I never could preserve—now mother does it, and for next to no money whatever. What nice dogs-in-a-blanket she'd make for the children! *What's dogs-in-the-blanket?* Oh, they're delicious—as dear mother makes 'em.

"Now, you *have* tasted her Irish stew, Caudle? You remember that? Come, you're not asleep—you remember that? And how fond you are of it! And I know I never have it made to please you! Well, what a relief to me it would be if dear mother was always at hand, that you might have a stew when you liked. What a load it would be off my mind.

"Again, for pickles! Not at all like anybody else's pickles. Her red cabbage—why it's as crisp as biscuit! And then her walnuts—and her all-sorts! Eh, Caudle? You know how you love pickles; and how we sometimes tiff about 'em? Now if dear mother was here, a word would never pass between us. And I'm sure nothing would make me happier, for—you're not asleep, Caudle?—for I can't bear to quarrel, can I, love?

"The children, too, are so fond of her! And she'd be such a help to me with 'em! I'm sure, with dear mother in the house, I shouldn't care a fig for measles, or anything of the sort. As a nurse, she's such a treasure!

"And at her time of life, what a needlewoman! And the darning and mending for the children, it really gets quite beyond me now, Caudle. Now, with mother at my hand, there wouldn't be a stitch wanted in the house.

"And then, when you're out late, Caudle—for I know you must be out late, sometimes; I can't expect you, of course, to be always at home—why then dear mother

MRS. CAUDLE'S DEAR MOTHER.

could sit up for you, and nothing would delight the dear soul half so much.

"And so, Caudle, love, I think dear mother had better come, don't you? Eh, Caudle? Now, you're not asleep darling; don't you think she'd better come? You say *No*? You say *No* again? *You won't have her*, you say; *You won't, that's flat*? Caudle—Cau-Cau-dle—Cau—dle——"

"Here Mrs. Caudle," says her husband, "suddenly went into tears; and I went to sleep."

59

Lecture XII

Mr. Caudle, Having Come Home a Little Late, Declares that Henceforth "He Will Have a Key"

"Upon my word, Mr. Caudle, I think it a waste of time to come to bed at all now! The cocks will be crowing in a minute. *Why did I sit up, then?* Because I choose to sit up—but that's my thanks. No, it's no use your talking, Caudle; I never *will* let the girl sit up for you; and there's an end. What do you say? *Why does she sit up with me, then?* That's quite a different matter. You don't suppose I'm going to sit up alone, do you? What do you say? *What's the use of two sitting up?* That's my business. No, Caudle, it's no such thing. I *don't* sit up because I may have the pleasure of talking about it; and you're an ungrateful, unfeeling creature, to say so. I sit up because I choose it; and if you don't come home all the night long—and 'twill soon come to that I've no doubt—still, I'll never go to bed, so don't think it.

"Oh, yes! the time runs away very pleasantly with you men at your clubs—selfish creatures! You can laugh, and sing, and tell stories, and never think of the clock; never think there's such a person as a wife belonging to you. It's nothing to you that a poor woman's sitting up, and telling the minutes, and seeing all sorts of things in the fire—and sometimes thinking that something dreadful has happened to you—more

61

MR. CAUDLE HASN'T A LATCHKEY.

fool she to care a straw about you!—this is all nothing. Oh no; when a woman's once married she's a slave—worse than a slave—and must bear it all!

"And what you men can find to talk about I can't think! Instead of a man sitting every night at home with his wife, and going to bed at a Christian hour—going to a club, to meet a set of people who don't care a button for him—it's monstrous! What do you say? *You only go once a week*? That's nothing at all to do with it: you might as well go every night; and I dare say you will soon. But if you do, you may get in as you can: *I* won't sit up for you, I can tell you.

"My health's being destroyed night after night, and—oh, don't say it's only once a week; I tell you that's nothing to do with it—if you had any eyes, you would see how ill I am; but you've no eyes for anybody

"WHAT'S IT TO YOU, IF I LIKE TO SIT UP?"

belonging to you: oh no! your eyes are for people out of doors. It's very well for you to call me a foolish, aggravating woman! I should like to see the woman who'd sit up for you as I do. *You didn't want me to sit up?* Yes, yes; that's your thanks—that's your gratitude: I'm to ruin my health, and to be abused for it. Nice principles you've got at that club, Mr. Caudle!

"But there's one comfort—one great comfort; it can't last long: I'm sinking—I feel it, though I never say anything about it—but I know my own feelings, and I say it can't last long. And then I should like to know who will sit up for you! Then I should like to know how your second wife—what do you say? *You'll never be troubled with another*? Troubled, indeed! *I* never troubled you, Caudle. No; it's you who've troubled me; and you know it; though like a foolish woman I've borne it all, and never said a word about it. But it *can't* last—that's one blessing.

"Oh, if a woman could only know what she'd have to suffer before she was married—Don't tell me you want to go to sleep! If you want to go to sleep, you should come home at proper hours! It's time to get up, for what I know now. Shouldn't wonder if you hear the milk in five minutes—there's the sparrows up already; yes, I say the sparrows; and, Caudle, you ought to blush to hear 'em. *You don't hear 'em*? Ha! you won't hear 'em, you mean: *I* hear 'em. No, Mr. Caudle; it *isn't* the wind whistling in the key-hole; I'm not quite foolish, though you may think so. I hope I know wind from a sparrow!

"Ha! when I think what a man you were before we were married! But you're now another person—quite an altered creature. But I suppose you're all alike—I dare say, every poor woman's troubled and put upon, though I should hope not so much as I am. Indeed, I should hope not! Going and staying out, and—

"What! *You'll have a key*? Will you! Not while I'm alive, Mr. Caudle. I'm not going to bed with the door upon the latch, for you or the best man breathing. *You won't have a latch—you'll have a Chubb's lock*? Will you? I'll have no Chubb here, I can tell you. What do you say? *You'll have the lock put on to-morrow*? Well, try it; that's all I say, Caudle; try it. I won't let you put me in a passion; but all I say is—try it.

"A respectable thing, that, for a married man to carry

about with him—a street-door key! That tells a tale, I think. A nice thing for the father of a family! A key! What, to let yourself in and out when you please! To come in, like a thief in the middle of the night, instead of knocking at the door like a decent person! Oh, don't tell me that you only want to prevent me sitting up—if I choose to sit up, what's that to you? Some wives, indeed, would make a noise about sitting up, but *you've* no reason to complain—goodness knows.

"Well, upon my word, I've lived to hear something. Carry the street-door key about with you! I've heard of such things with young good-for-nothing bachelors, with nobody to care what became of 'em; but for a married man to leave his wife and children in a house, with the door upon the latch—don't talk to me about Chubb, it's all the same—a great deal you must care for us. Yes, it's very well for you to say, that you only want the key for peace and quietness—what's it to you, if I like to sit up? You've no business to complain; it can't distress you. Now, it's no use your talking; all I say is this, Caudle: if you send a man to put on any lock here, I'll call in a policeman; as I'm your married wife, I will!

"No, I think when a man comes to have the street-door key, the sooner he turns bachelor altogether the better. I'm sure, Caudle, I don't want to be any clog upon you. Now, it's no use your telling me to hold my tongue, for I—What? *I give you the headache, do I*? No, I don't, Caudle; it's your club that gives you the headache: it's your smoke, and your—well! if ever I knew such a man in all my life! there's no saying a word to you! You go out, and treat yourself like an emperor—and come home at twelve at night, or any hour for what I know and—then you threaten to have a key, and—and—and——"

"I *did* get to sleep at last," said Caudle, "amidst the failing sentences of 'take children into a lodging'—'separate maintenance'—'won't be made a slave of'—and so forth."

*Mrs. Caudle Has Been to See her Dear
Mother. Caudle, on the "Joyful
Occasion", Has Given a Party, and Issued
the Subjoined Card of Invitation*

*Mr. Caudle's compliments to Mr. Henry Prettyman, and
expects to have the honour of his company on this joyful
occasion, at half-past Eight o'Clock.*

"It *is* hard, I think, Mr. Caudle, that I can't leave home
for a day or two, but the house must be turned into a
tavern: a tavern?—a pot-house! Yes, I thought you were
very anxious that I should go; I thought you wanted to
get rid of me for something, or you would not have
insisted on my staying at dear mother's all night. You
were afraid I should get cold coming home, were you?
Oh yes, you can be very tender, you can, Mr. Caudle,
when it suits your own purpose. Yes! and the world

thinks what a good husband you are! I only wish the world knew you as well as I do, that's all; but it shall, some day, I'm determined.

"I'm sure the house will not be sweet for a month. All the curtains are poisoned with smoke; and, what's more, with the filthiest smoke I ever knew. *Take 'em down, then?* Yes it's all very well for you to say, take 'em down; but they were only cleaned and put up a month ago; but a careful wife's lost upon you, Mr. Caudle. You ought to have married somebody who'd have let your house go to wreck and ruin, as I will for the future. People who don't care for their families are better thought of than those who do; I've long found out *that*.

MR. CAUDLE HAS INVITED A FEW FRIENDS TO SUPPER.

"And what a condition the carpet's in! They've taken five pounds out of it, if a farthing, with their filthy boots, and I don't know what besides. And then the smoke in the hearthrug, and a large cinder hole burnt in it! I never saw such a house in *my* life! If you wanted to have a few friends, why couldn't you invite 'em when your wife's at home, like any other man? not have 'em sneaking in, like a set of housebreakers, directly a woman turns her back. They must be pretty gentlemen, they must; mean fellows, that are afraid to face a woman! Ha! and you all call yourselves the lords of the creation! I should only like to see what would become of the creation, if you were left to yourselves! A pretty pickle creation would be in very soon!

"You must all have been in a nice condition? What do you say? *You took nothing?* Took nothing, didn't you? I'm sure there's such a regiment of empty bottles, I haven't had the heart to count 'em. And punch, too! you must have punch! There's a hundred half-lemons in the kitchen, if there's one; for Susan, like a good girl, kept 'em to show 'em me. No, sir; Susan s*han't leave the house!* What do you say? *She has no right to tell tales, and you* WILL *be master of your own house?* Will you? If you don't alter, Mr. Caudle, you'll soon have no house to be master of. A whole loaf of sugar did I leave in the cupboard, and now there isn't as much as would fill a tea-cup. Do you suppose I'm to find sugar for punch for fifty men? What do you say? *There wasn't fifty?* That's no matter; the more shame for 'em, sir. I'm sure they drunk enough for fifty. Do you suppose out of my housekeeping money I'm to find sugar for punch for all the world? *You don't ask me?* Don't you ask me? You do; you know you do; for if I only want a shilling extra, the house is in a blaze. And yet a whole loaf of sugar can you throw away upon—No, I *won't* be still: and I *won't* let you go to sleep. If you'd got to bed at a proper hour last night, you wouldn't have been so sleepy now. You can sit up half the night with a pack of people who don't care for you, and your poor wife can't get in a word!

"And there's that China image that I had when I was married—I wouldn't have taken any sum of money for it, and you know it—and how do I find it? With its precious head knocked off! And what was more mean, more contemptible than all besides, it was put on again, as if nothing had happened. *You knew nothing about it?* Now, how can you lie there, in your Christian bed, Caudle, and say that? You know that that fellow, Prettyman, knocked off the head with the poker? You know that he did. And you hadn't the feeling—yes, I will say it—you hadn't the feeling to protect what you knew was precious to me. Oh no, if the truth was known, you were glad to see it broken for that very reason.

"Every way, I've been insulted. I should like to know who it was who corked whiskers on my dear aunt's picture? Oh! you're laughing, are you? *You're not laughing?* Don't tell me that. I should like to know what shakes the bed, then, if you're not laughing? Yes, corked whiskers on her dear face—and she was a good soul to you, Caudle, and you ought to be ashamed of yourself to see her ill-used. Oh, you may laugh! It's very easy to laugh! I only wish you'd a little feeling, like other people, that's all.

"Then there's my china mug—the mug I had before I was married—when I was a happy creature. I should like to know who knocked the spout off that mug? Don't tell me it was cracked before—it's no such thing,

70

"YES, CORKED WHISKERS ON HER DEAR FACE."

Caudle; there wasn't a flaw in it—and now, I could have cried when I saw it. Don't tell me it wasn't worth two-pence. How do you know? You never buy mugs. But that's like men; they think nothing in a house costs anything.

"There's four glasses broke and nine cracked. At least, that's all I've found out at present; but I dare say I shall discover a dozen to-morrow.

"And I should like to know where the cotton umbrella's gone to—and I should like to know who broke the bell-pull—and perhaps you don't know there's a leg off a chair—and perhaps—"

"I was resolved," says Caudle, "to know nothing, and so went to sleep in my ignorance."

Mrs. Caudle Thinks it "High Time" that the Children Should Have Summer Clothing

"If there's anything in the world I hate—and you know it, Caudle—it is asking you for money. I am sure, for myself, I'd rather go without a thing a thousand times, and I do—the more shame of you to let me, but—there, now! there you fly out again! *What do I want now?* Why, you must know what's wanted if you'd any eyes—or any pride for your children like any other father. *What's the matter—and what am I driving at?* Oh, nonsense, Caudle! As if you didn't know! I'm sure if I'd any money of my own, I'd never ask you for a farthing: never; it's painful to me, goodness knows! What do you say? *If it's painful, why so often do it?* Ha! I suppose you call that a joke—one of your club jokes! I wish you'd think a little more of people's feelings, and less of your jokes. As I say, I only wish I'd any money of my own. If there is anything that humbles a poor woman, it is coming to a man's pocket for every farthing. It's dreadful!

"Now, Caudle, if ever you kept awake, you shall keep awake to-night—yes, you shall hear me, for it isn't often I speak, and then you may go to sleep as soon as you like. Pray do you know what month it is? And did you see how the children looked at church to-day—like

73

nobody else's children? *What was the matter with them?* Oh, Caudle! How can you ask? Poor things! weren't they all in their thick merinoes, and beaver bonnets! What do you say—*What of it?* What! you'll tell me that you didn't see how the Briggs's girls, in their new chips, turned their noses up at 'em? And you didn't see how the Browns looked at the Smiths, and then at our dear girls, as much as to say, 'Poor creatures; what figures for the month of May!' *You didn't see it?* The more shame for you—you would if you'd had the feelings of a parent— but I'm sorry to say, Caudle, you haven't. I'm sure those Briggs's girls—the little minxes!—put me into such a pucker, I could have pulled their ears for 'em over the pew. What do you say? *I ought to be ashamed of myself to own it?* No, Mr. Caudle: the shame lies with you, that don't let your children appear at church like other people's children; that make 'em uncomfortable at their devotions, poor things; for how can it be otherwise, when they see themselves dressed like nobody else?

"Now, Caudle, it's no use talking; those children shall not cross the threshold next Sunday if they haven't things for the summer. Now mind—they shan't; and there's an end of it. I won't have 'em exposed to the Briggses and the Browns again: no, they shall know they have a mother, if they've no father to feel for 'em. What do you say, Caudle? *A good deal I must think of church, if I think so much of what we go in?* I only wish you thought as much as I do, you'd be a better man than you are, Caudle, I can tell you; but that's nothing to do with it. I'm talking about decent clothes for the children for the summer, and you want to put me off with something about the church; but that's so like you, Caudle!

"*I'm always wanting money for clothes?* How can you lie in your bed and say that? I'm sure there's no children in the world that cost their father so little: but that's it; the less a poor woman does upon, the less she may. It's the wives who don't care where the money comes from who're best thought of. Oh, if my time was to come over again, would I mend and stitch, and make the things go so far as I have done? No—that I wouldn't. Yes, it's very well for you to lie there and laugh; it's easy to laugh, Caudle—very easy, to people who don't feel.

"Now, Caudle, dear! What a man you are! I know you'll give me the money, because, after all, I think you love your children, and like to see 'em well dressed. It's only natural that a father should. Eh, Caudle, eh! Now you shan't go to sleep till you've told me. *How much money do I want?* Why, let me see, love. There's Caroline, and Jane, and Susannah, and Mary Anne, and—What do you say? *I needn't count 'em, you know how many there are?* Ha! that's just as you take me up. Well, how much money will it take? Let me see; and don't go to sleep. I'll tell you in a minute. You always love to see the dear things like new pins, I know that, Caudle; and though I say it—bless their little hearts!—they do credit to you, Caudle. Any nobleman of the land might be proud of 'em. Now don't swear at noblemen of the land, and ask me what they've to do with your children; you know what I meant. But you *are* so hasty, Caudle.

"*How much?* Now, don't be in a hurry! Well, I think, with good pinching—and you know, Caudle, there's never a wife who can pinch closer than I can—I think, with pinching, I can do with twenty pounds. What did you say? *Twenty fiddlesticks?* What? *You won't give half the money?* Very well, Mr. Caudle; I don't care: let the

"TWENTY POUNDS I WILL HAVE, MR. CAUDLE IF I'VE ANY."

children go in rags; let them stop from church, and grow up like heathens and cannibals, and then you'll save your money, and, I suppose, be satisfied. *You gave me twenty pounds five months ago!* What's five months ago to do with now? Besides, what I *have* had is nothing to do with it.

"What do you say? *Ten pounds are enough?* Yes: just like you men; you think things cost nothing for women; but you don't care how much you lay out upon yourselves. *They only want bonnets and frocks?* How do you know what they want? *How* should a man know anything at all about it? And you won't give more than ten pounds? Very well. Then you may go shopping with it yourself, and see what *you'll* make of it. I'll have none of your ten pounds, I can tell you. No, sir—no; you have no cause to say that. *I don't want to dress the children up like countesses?* You often fling that in my teeth, you do: but you know it's false, Caudle; you know it. I only want to give 'em proper notions of themselves: and what, indeed, *can* the poor things think when they see the Briggses, and the Browns, and the Smiths—and their fathers don't make the money you do, Caudle—when they see them as fine as tulips? Why they must think themselves nobody; and to think yourself nobody—depend upon it, Caudle—isn't the way to make the world think anything of you.

"What do you say? *Where did I pick up that?* Where do you think. I know a great deal more than you suppose—yes; though you don't give me credit for it. Husbands seldom do. However, the twenty pounds I *will* have, if I've any—or not a farthing.

"No, sir, no. *I don't want to dress up the children like peacocks and parrots*! I only want to make 'em respectable and—what do you say? *You'll give fifteen pounds?* No, Caudle, no—not a penny will I take under twenty; if I did, it would seem as if I wanted to waste your money: and I'm sure, when I come to think of it, twenty pounds will hardly do. Still, if you'll give me twenty— no, it's no use your offering fifteen, and wanting to go to sleep. You shan't close an eye until you promise the twenty. Come, Caudle, love!—twenty, and then you may go to sleep. Twenty—twenty—twenty—"

"My impression is," writes Caudle, "that I fell asleep sticking firmly to the fifteen; but in the morning Mrs. Caudle assured me, as a woman of honour, that she wouldn't let me wink an eye, before I promised the twenty: and man is frail—and woman is strong—she had the money."

Mr. Caudle Has Again Stayed Out Late. Mrs. Caudle, at First Injured and Violent, Melts

"Perhaps, Mr. Caudle, you'll tell me where this is to end? Though, goodness knows, I needn't ask *that*. The end is plain enough. Out—out—out! Every night—every night! I'm sure men who can't come home at reasonable hours have no business with wives: they have no right to destroy other people, if they choose to go to destruction themselves. Ha, lord! Oh, dear! I only hope none of my girls will ever marry—I hope they'll none of 'em ever be the slave their poor mother is: they shan't if I can help it. What do you say? *Nothing*? Well, I don't wonder at that, Mr. Caudle; you ought to be ashamed to speak; I don't wonder that you can't open your mouth. I'm only astonished that at such hours you have the confidence to knock at your own door. Though I'm your wife, I must say it, I do sometimes wonder at your impudence. What do you say? *Nothing*? Ha! you are an aggravating creature, Caudle; lying there like the mummy of a man, and never as much as opening your lips to one. Just as if your own wife wasn't worth answering! It isn't so when you're out I'm sure. Oh, no! then you can talk fast enough; here, there's no getting a word from you. But you treat your wife as no other man does—and you know it.

"Out—out every night! What? *You haven't been out this week before?* That's nothing at all to do with it. You might just as well be out all the week as once—just! And I should like to know what could keep you out till these hours? *Business?* Oh, yes—I dare say! Pretty business a married man and the father of a family must have out of doors at one in the morning. What! *I shall drive you mad?* Oh, no; you haven't feelings enough to go mad—you'd be a better man, Caudle, if you had. *Will I listen to you?* What's the use? Of course you've some story to put me off with—you can all do that, and laugh at us afterwards.

MR. CAUDLE HAS A MIDNIGHT VISITOR.

"No, Caudle, don't say that. I'm not always trying to find fault—not I. It's you. I never speak but when there's occasion; and what in my time I've put up with, there isn't anybody in the world that knows. *Will I hear your story*? Oh, you may tell it if you please; go on: only mind, I shan't believe a word of it. I'm not such a fool as other women are, I can tell you. There, now—don't begin to swear—but go on——

"—And that's your story, is it? That's your excuse for the hours you keep! That's your apology for under-mining my health and ruining your family! What do you think your children will say of you when they grow up—going and throwing away your money upon good-for-nothing pot-house acquaintance? *He's not a pot-house acquaintance*? Who is he, then? Come, you haven't told me that; but I know, it's that Prettyman! Yes, to be sure it is! Upon my life! Well, if I've hardly patience to lie in the same bed! I've wanted a silver teapot these five years, and you must go and throw away as much money as—what! *You haven't thrown it away*? Haven't you? Then my name's not Margaret, that's all I know!

"A man gets arrested, and because he's taken from his wife and family, and locked up, you must go and trouble your head with it! And you must be mixing yourself up with nasty sheriff's officers—pah! I'm sure you're not fit to enter a decent house—and go running from lawyer to lawyer to get bail, and settle the business, as you call it! A pretty settlement you'll make of it—mark my words! Yes—and to mend the matter, to finish it quite, you must be one of the bail! That any man who isn't a born fool should do such a thing for another! Do you think anybody would do as much for you? *Yes*? You say yes? Well, I only wish—just to show that I'm right—I only wish you were in a condition to try 'em. I should only like to see you arrested. You'd find the difference—*that* you would.

"What's other people's affairs to you? If you were

locked up, depend upon it, there's not a soul would come near you. No; it's all very fine now, when people think there isn't a chance of your being in trouble—but I should only like to see what they'd say to you if *you* were in a sponging-house. Yes—I should enjoy *that* just to show you that I'm always right. What do you say? *You think better of the world?* Ha! that would be all very well if you could afford it; but you're not in means, I know, to think so well of people as all that. And of course they only laugh at you. 'Caudle's an easy fool,' they cry—I know it as well as if I heard 'em—'Caudle's an easy fool, anybody may lead him.' Yes; anybody but his own wife—and she—of course—is nobody.

"And now everybody that's arrested will of course send to you. Yes, Mr. Caudle, you'll have your hands full now, no doubt of it. You'll soon know every sponging-house and every sheriff's officer in London. Your business will have to take care of itself; you'll have enough to do to run from lawyer to lawyer after the business of other people. Now, it's no use calling me a dear soul—not a bit! No; and I shan't put it off till to-morrow. It isn't often I speak, but I *will* speak now.

"I wish that Prettyman had been at the bottom of the sea before—what? *It isn't Prettyman?* Ha! it's very well for you to say so; but I know it is; it's just like him. He looks like a man that's always in debt—that's always in a sponging-house. Anybody might swear it. I knew it from the first time you brought him here—from the very night he put his nasty dirty wet boots on my bright steel fender. Any woman could see what the fellow was in a minute. Prettyman! A pretty gentleman, truly, to be robbing your wife and family!

"Why couldn't you let him stop in the sponging——

MR. CAUDLE IS CALLED TO A SPONGING-HOUSE.

Now don't call upon Heaven in that way, and ask me to
be quiet, for I won't. Why couldn't you let him stop
there? He got himself in; he might have got himself out
again. And you must keep me awake, ruin my sleep, my
health, and, for what you care, my peace of mind. Ha!
everybody but you can see how I'm breaking. You can
do all this while you're talking with a set of low bailiffs!
A great deal you must think of your children to go into a
lawyer's office.

"And then you must be bail—you must be bound—

83

for Mr. Prettyman! You may say, bound! Yes—you've
your hands nicely tied, now. How he laughs at you—
and serve you right! Why, in another week he'll be in
the East Indies; of course, he will! And you'll have to
pay his debts; yes, your children may go in rags, so that
Mr. Prettyman—what do you say? *It isn't Prettyman?* I
know better. Well, if it isn't Prettyman that's kept you
out—if it isn't Prettyman you're bail for, who is it then?
I ask, who is it then? What! *My brother? Brother Tom?*
Oh, Caudle! dear Caudle—"

"It was too much for the poor soul," says Caudle;
"she sobbed as if her heart would break, and I"—and
here the MS. is blotted, as though Caudle himself had
dropt tears as he wrote.

Lecture XVI

Baby Is to Be Christened; Mrs. Caudle Canvasses the Merits of Probable Godfathers

"Come, now, love, about baby's name? The dear thing's three months old, and not a name to its back yet. There you go again! Talk of it to-morrow! No; we'll talk of it to-night. There's no having a word with you in the day-time—but here you can't leave me. Now don't say you wish you could, Caudle; that's unkind, and not treating a wife—especially the wife I am to you—as she deserves. It isn't often that I speak; but I *do* believe you'd like never to hear the sound of my voice. I might as well have been born dumb!

"I suppose the baby *must* have a godfather; and so, Caudle, who shall we have? Who do you think will be able to do the most for it? No, Caudle, no: I'm not a selfish woman—nothing of the sort—but I hope I've the feelings of a mother; and what's the use of a godfather, if he gives nothing else to the child but a name? A child might almost as well not be christened at all. And so who shall we have? What do you say? *Anybody*? Ar'n't you ashamed of yourself, Caudle? Don't you think something will happen to you, to talk in that way? I don't know where you pick up such principles. I'm thinking who there is among our acquaintance who can do the most for the blessed

creature, and you say—'*Anybody*!' Caudle, you're quite
a heathen.

"There's Wagstaff. No chance of his ever marrying,
and he's very fond of babies. He's plenty of money,
Caudle; and I think he might be got. Babies, I know it—
babies are his weak side. Wouldn't it be a blessed thing
to find our dear child in his will? Why don't you speak?
I declare, Caudle, you seem to care no more for the
child than if it was a stranger's. People who can't love
children more than you do, ought never to have 'em.
You don't like Wagstaff? No more do I much; but what's
that to do with it? People who've their families to
provide for, mustn't think of their feelings. *I* don't like
him; but then I'm a mother, and love my baby! *You
won't have Wagstaff, and that's flat*? Ha, Caudle, you're
like nobody else—not fit for this world, you're not.

"What do you think of Pugsby? I can't bear his wife;
but that's nothing to do with it. *I* know my duty to my
babe: I wish other people did. What do you say?
Pugsby's a wicked fellow? Ha! that's like you—always
giving people a bad name. We mustn't always believe
what the world says, Caudle; it doesn't become us as
Christians to do it. I only know that he hasn't chick or
child; and, besides that, he's a very strong interest in
the Blue-coats; and so, if Pugsby——Now, don't fly out
at the man in that manner. Caudle, you ought to be
ashamed of yourself! You can't speak well of anybody.
Where *do* you think to go to?

"What do you say then to Sniggins? Now don't
bounce round in that way, letting the cold air in the bed!
What's the matter with Sniggins? *You wouldn't ask him
a favour for the world*? Well, it's a good thing the baby
has somebody to care for it: *I* will. What do you say? *I*

shan't? I will, I can tell you. Sniggins, besides being a warm man, has good interest in the Customs; and there's nice pickings there, if one only goes the right way to get 'em. It's no use, Caudle, your fidgeting about—not a bit. I'm not going to have baby lost— sacrificed, I may say, like its brothers and sisters. *What do I mean by sacrificed*? Oh, you know what I mean very well. What have any of 'em got by their godfathers beyond a half-pint mug, a knife and fork, and spoon— and a shabby coat, that I know was bought second-hand, for I could almost swear to the place? And then there was your fine friend Hartley's wife—what did she give to Caroline? Why, a trumpery lace cap it made me blush to look at. What? *It was the best she could afford*? Then she'd no right to stand for the child. People who can't do better than that have no business to take the responsibility of godmother. They ought to know their duties better.

"Well, Caudle, you can't object to Goldman? *Yes, you do*! Was there ever such a man! What for? *He's a usurer and a hunks*? Well, I'm sure, you've no business in this world, Caudle; you have such high-flown notions. Why isn't the man as rich as the bank? And as for his being a usurer—isn't it all the better for those that come after him? I'm sure it's well there's some people in the world who save money, seeing the stupid creatures who throw it away. But you are the strangest man! I really believe you think money a sin, instead of the greatest blessing; for I can't mention any of our acquaintance that's rich—and I'm sure we don't know too many such people—that you haven't something to say against 'em. It's only beggars that you like—people with not a shilling to bless themselves. Ha! though you're my husband, I must say it—you're a man of low notions, Caudle. I only hope none of the dear boys will take after their father.

"And I should like to know what's the objection to Goldman? The only thing against him is his name; I must confess it, I don't like the name of Lazarus: it's low and doesn't sound genteel—not at all respectable. But, after he's gone and done what's proper for the child, the boy could easily slip Lazarus into Laurence. I'm told the thing's done often. No, Caudle, don't say that—I'm not a mean woman; certainly not; quite the reverse. I've only a parent's love for my children; and I must say it—I wish everybody felt as I did.

"I suppose, if the truth was known, you'd like your tobacco-pipe friend, your pot-companion, Prettyman, to stand for the child? *You'd have no objection?* I thought not! Yes; I knew what it was coming to. He's a beggar, he is; and a person who stays out half the night; yes, he does; and it's no use your denying it—a beggar and tippler, and that's the man you'd make godfather to your own flesh and blood! Upon my word, Caudle, it's enough to make a woman get up and dress herself to hear you talk.

"Well, I can hardly tell you, if you won't have Wagstaff, or Pugsby, or Sniggins, or Goldman, or somebody that's respectable, to do what's proper, the child shan't be christened at all. As for Prettyman, or any such riffraff—no, never! I'm sure there's a certain set of people that poverty's catching from, and that Prettyman's one of 'em. Now, Caudle, I won't have my dear child lost by any of your spittoon acquaintance, I can tell you.

"No; unless I can have *my* way, the child shan't be

christened at all. What do you say? *It must have a name?*
There's no 'must' at all in the case—none. No: it shall
have no name; and then see what the world will say. I'll
call it Number Six—yes, that will do as well as anything
else, unless I've the godfather I like. Number Six
Caudle! ha! ha! I think that must make you ashamed of
yourself if anything can. Number Six Caudle—a much
better name than Mr. Prettyman could give! yes,
Number Six! What do you say? *Anything but Number
Seven?* Oh, Caudle, if ever—"

"At this moment," writes Caudle, "little Number Six
began to cry; and taking advantage of the happy
accident, I somehow got to sleep."

Lecture XVII

Caudle in the Course of the Day Has Ventured to Question the Economy of "Washing at Home"

"A pretty temper you come to bed in, Mr. Caudle, I can see! Oh, don't deny it—I think I ought to know by this time. But it's always the way; whenever I get up a few things, the house can hardly hold you! Nobody cries out more about clean linen than you do—and nobody leads a poor woman so miserable a life when she tries to make her husband comfortable. Yes, Mr. Caudle— comfortable! You needn't keep chewing the word, as if you couldn't swallow it. *Was there ever such a woman?* No, Caudle; I hope not: I should hope no other wife was ever put upon as I am! It's all very well for you. I can't have a little wash at home like anybody else, but you must go about the house swearing to yourself, and looking at your wife as if she was your bitterest enemy. But I suppose you'd rather we didn't wash at all. Yes; then you'd be happy! To be sure you would—you'd like to have all the children in their dirt, like potatoes: anything, so that it didn't disturb you. I wish you'd had a wife who'd never washed—*she'd* have suited you, she would. Yes: a fine lady who'd have let your children go that you might have scraped 'em. She'd have been much better cared for than I am. I only wish I could let all of you go without clean linen at all—yes, all of you. I wish I could! And if I wasn't a slave to my family, unlike anybody else, I should.

"No, Mr. Caudle; the house isn't tossed about in water as if it was Noah's Ark! And you ought to be ashamed of yourself to talk of Noah's Ark in that loose manner. I'm sure I don't know what I've done to be married to a man of such principles. No: and the whole house *doesn't* taste of soap-suds either; and if it did, any other man but yourself would be above naming it. I suppose I don't like washing-day any more than yourself. What do you say? *Yes I do*? Ha! you're wrong

MR. CAUDLE THINKS THE HOUSE TASTES OF SOAP-SUDS.

there, Mr. Caudle. No; I don't like it because it makes everybody else uncomfortable. No; and I ought not to have been born a mermaid, that I might always have been in water. A mermaid, indeed! What next will you call me? But no man, Mr. Caudle, says such things to his wife as you. However, as I've said before, it can't last long, that's one comfort. What do you say? *You're glad of it?* You're a brute, Mr. Caudle! No, you *didn't* mean washing: I know what you meant. A pretty speech to a woman who's been the wife to you I have! You'll repent it when it's too late: yes, I wouldn't have your feelings when I'm gone, Caudle; no, not for the Bank of England.

"And when we only wash once a fortnight! Ha! I only wish you had some wives: they'd wash once a week! Besides, if once a fortnight's too much for you, why don't you give me money that we may have things to go a month? Is it *my* fault, if we're short? What do you say? *My 'once a fortnight' lasts three days?* No, it doesn't; never; well, very seldom, and that's the same thing. Can I help it, if the blacks will fly, and the things must be rinsed again? Don't say that: I'm *not* made happy by the blacks, and they *don't* prolong my enjoyment: and, more than that, you're an unfeeling man to say so. You're enough to make a woman wish herself in her grave—you are, Caudle.

"And a pretty example you set to your sons! Because we'd a little wash to-day, and there wasn't a hot dinner—and who thinks of getting anything hot for washer-women?—because you hadn't everything as you always have it, you must swear at the cold mutton—and you don't know what that mutton cost a pound, I dare say—you must swear at a sweet wholesome joint like a lord. What? *You didn't swear?* Yes; it's very well for you to say so; but I know when you're swearing; and you swear when you little think it; and I say you must go on swearing as you did, and seize your hat like a savage, and rush out of the house, and go and take your dinner at a tavern! A pretty wife people must think you have, when they find you dining at a public-house. A nice home they must think you have, Mr. Caudle! What! *You'll do so every time I wash?* Very well, Mr. Caudle—very well. We'll soon see who's tired of that, first; for I'll wash a stocking a day if that's all, sooner than you should have everything as you like. Ha! that's so like you: you'd trample everybody under foot, if you could—you know you would, Caudle, so don't deny it.

"Now, if you begin to shout in that manner, I'll leave the bed. It's very hard that I can't say a single word to you, but you must almost raise the place. *You didn't shout?* I don't know what you call shouting, then! I'm sure the people must hear you in the next house. No—it won't do to call me soft names, now, Caudle: I'm not the fool that I was when I was first married—I know better now. You're to treat me in the manner you have, all day; and then at night, the only time and place when I can get a word in, you want to go to sleep. How can you be so mean, Caudle?

"What! *Why can't I put the washing out?* Now, you have asked that a thousand times, but it's no use, Caudle; so don't ask it again. I won't put it out. What do you say? *Mrs. Prettyman says it's quite as cheap?* Pray, what's Mrs. Prettyman to me? I should think, Mr. Caudle, that I know very well how to take care of my family, without Mrs. Prettyman's advice. Mrs. Prettyman, indeed! I only wish she'd come here, that I might tell her so! Mrs. Prettyman! But, perhaps she'd better come and take care of your house for you! Oh, yes! I've no doubt she'd do it much better than I do—*much*. No, Caudle! *I won't hold my tongue.* I think I ought to be mistress of my own washing by this time—and after the wife I've been to you, it's cruel of you to go on as you do.

"Don't tell me about putting the washing out. I say it isn't so cheap—I don't care whether you wash by the dozen or not—it isn't so cheap; I've reduced everything, and I save at least a shilling a week. What do you say? *A trumpery shilling?* Ha! I only hope to goodness you'll not come to want, talking of shillings in the way you do. Now, don't begin about your comfort: don't go on aggravating me, and asking me if your comfort's not worth a shilling a week? That's nothing at all to do with it—nothing: but that's your way—when I talk of one thing, you talk of another; that's so like you men, and you know it. Allow me to tell you, Mr. Caudle, that a shilling a week is two pound twelve a year, and take two pound twelve a year for, let us say, thirty years, and—well you needn't groan, Mr. Caudle—I don't suppose it will be so long; oh, no! you'll have somebody else to look after your washing long before that—and if it wasn't for my dear children's sake I shouldn't care how soon. You know my mind—and so, good night, Mr. Caudle."

"Thankful for her silence," writes Caudle, "I was fast dropping to sleep; when, jogging my elbow, my wife observed—'Mind, there's the cold mutton to-morrow—nothing hot till that's gone. Remember, too, as it was a short wash to-day, we wash again on Wednesday.'"

Lecture XVIII

Caudle, Whilst Walking with his Wife, Has Been Bowed to by a Younger and Even Prettier Woman than Mrs. Caudle

"If I'm not to leave the house without being insulted, Mr. Caudle, I had better stay indoors all my life.

"What! Don't tell me to let you have *one* night's rest! I wonder at your impudence! It's mighty fine, I never can go out with you, and—goodness knows!—it's seldom enough, without having my feelings torn to

MRS. CAUDLE "WONDERS AT HIS IMPUDENCE".

97

pieces by people of all sorts. A set of bold minxes! *What am I raving about?* Oh, you know very well—very well, indeed, Mr. Caudle. A pretty person she must be to nod to a man walking with his own wife! Don't tell me that it's Miss Prettyman—what's Miss Prettyman to me? Oh! *You've met her once or twice at her brother's house?* Yes, I dare say you have—no doubt of it. I always thought there was something very tempting about that house—and now I know it all. Now, it's no use, Mr. Caudle, your beginning to talk loud, and twist and toss your arms about as if you were as innocent as a born babe—I'm not to be deceived by such tricks now. No; there was a time, when I was a fool and believed anything; but—I thank my stars!—I've got over that.

"A bold minx! You suppose I didn't see her laugh, too, when she nodded to you! Oh yes, I knew what she thought me; a poor miserable creature, of course. I could see that. No—don't say so, Caudle. I *don't* always see more than anybody else—but I can't and won't be blind, however agreeable it might be to you; I must have

AN EVEN PRETTIER WOMAN THAN MRS. CAUDLE

the use of my senses. I'm sure, if a woman wants attention and respect from a man, she'd better be anything than his wife. I've always thought so; and to-day's decided it.

"No; I'm not ashamed of myself to talk so—certainly not. *A good amiable young creature, indeed!* Yes; I dare say; very amiable, no doubt. Of course, you think her so. You suppose I didn't see what sort of a bonnet she had on? Oh, a very good creature! And you think I didn't see the smudges of court-plaster about her face? *You didn't see 'em?* Very likely; but I did. Very amiable, to be sure! What do you say? *I made her blush at my ill-manners?* I should like to have seen her blush! 'Twould have been rather difficult, Mr. Caudle, for a blush to come through all that paint. No—I'm not a censorious woman, Mr. Caudle; quite the reverse. No; and you may threaten to get up, if you like—I will speak. I know what colour is, and I say it *was* paint. I believe, Mr. Caudle, *I* once had a complexion; though, of course, you've quite forgotten that: I think I once had a colour, before your conduct destroyed it. Before I knew you, people used to call me the Lily and Rose; but—what are you laughing at? I see nothing to laugh at. But as I say, anybody before your own wife.

"And I can't walk out with you but you're bowed to by every woman you meet! *What do I mean by every woman, when it's only Miss Prettyman?* That's nothing at all to do with it. How do I know who bows to you when I'm not by? Everybody of course. And if they don't look at you, why you look at them. Oh! I'm sure you do. You do it even when I'm out with you, and of course you do it when I'm away. Now, don't tell me, Caudle—don't deny it. The fact is, it's become such a dreadful habit with you, that you don't know when you do it, and when you don't. But I do.

"Miss Prettyman, indeed! What do you say? *You won't lie still and hear me scandalise that excellent young woman*? Oh, of course, you'll take her part! Though, to be sure, she may not be so much to blame after all. For how is she to know you're married? You're never seen out of doors with your own wife—never. Wherever you go, you go alone. Of course people think you're a bachelor. What do you say? *You well know you're not*? That's nothing to do with it—I only ask what must people think, when I'm never seen with you? Other women go out with their husbands: but as I've often said, I'm not like any other woman. What are you sneering at, Mr. Caudle? *How do I know you're sneering*? Don't tell me: I know well enough, by the movement of the pillow.

"No; you never take me out—and you know it. No; and it's not my own fault. How can you lie there and say that? Oh, a poor excuse! That's what you always say. You're tired of asking me, indeed, because I always start some objection? Of course I can't go out a figure. And when you ask me to go, you know very well that my bonnet isn't as it should be—or that my gown hasn't come home—or that I can't leave the children—or that something keeps me in-doors. You know all this, well enough before you ask me. And that's your art. And when I *do* go out with you I'm sure to suffer for it. Yes; you needn't repeat my words. *Suffer for it*. But you suppose I have no feelings: oh no, nobody has feelings but yourself. Yes; I'd forgot: Miss Prettyman, perhaps —yes, she may have feelings, of course.

"And as I've said, I dare say a pretty dupe people

think me. To be sure; a poor forlorn creature I must look in everybody's eyes. But I knew you couldn't be at Mr. Prettyman's house night after night till eleven o'clock—and a great deal you thought of me sitting up for you—I knew you couldn't be there without some cause. And now I've found it out! Oh, I don't mind your swearing, Mr. Caudle! It's I, if I wasn't a woman, who ought to swear. But it's like you men. Lords of the creation, as you call yourselves! Lords, indeed! And pretty slaves you make of the poor creatures who are tied to you. But I'll be separated, Caudle; I will; and then I'll take care and let all the world know how you've used me. What do you say? *I may say my worst?* Ha! don't you tempt any woman in that way—don't Caudle; for I wouldn't answer for what I said.

"Miss Prettyman, indeed, and—oh yes! now I see! Now the whole light breaks in upon me! Now, I know why you wished me to ask her with Mr. and Mrs. Prettyman to tea! And I, like a poor blind fool, was nearly doing it. But now, I say, as my eyes are open! And you'd have brought her under my own roof—now it's no use your bouncing about in that fashion—you'd have brought her into the very house, where——"

"Here," says Caudle, "I could endure it no longer. So I jumped out of bed, and went and slept somehow with the children."

Lecture XIX

Mrs. Caudle Thinks "It Would Look Well to Keep Their Wedding-Day"

"Caudle, love, do you know what next Sunday is? *No! you don't?* Well, was there ever such a strange man! Can't you guess, darling? Next Sunday, dear? Think, love, a minute—just think. *What! and you don't know now?* Ha! if I hadn't a better memory than you, I don't know how we should ever get on. Well, then, pet—shall I tell you what next Sunday is? Why, then, it's our wedding-day——What are you groaning at, Mr. Caudle? I don't see anything to groan at. If anybody should groan, I'm sure it isn't you. No: I rather think it's I who ought to groan!

"Oh, dear! That's fourteen years ago. You were a very different man, then, Mr. Caudle. What do you say?—*And I was a very different woman?* Not at all—just the same. Oh, you needn't roll your head about on the pillow in that way: I say, just the same. Well, then, if I'm altered, whose fault is it? Not mine, I'm sure—certainly not. Don't tell me that I couldn't talk at all then—I could talk just as well then as I can now; only then I hadn't the same cause. It's you who've made me talk. What do you say? *You're very sorry for it?* Caudle, you do nothing but insult me.

"Ha! you were a good-tempered, nice creature fourteen years ago, and would have done anything for

103

MRS. CAUDLE'S WEDDING-DAY.

me. Yes, yes, if a woman would be always cared for, she should never marry. There's quite an end of the charm when she goes to church! We're all angels while you're courting us; but once married, how soon you pull our wings off! No, Mr. Caudle, I'm not talking nonsense; but the truth is, you like to hear nobody talk but yourself. Nobody ever tells me that I talk nonsense but you. Now, it's no use your turning and turning about in that way, it's not a bit of—what do you say? *You'll get up*? No, you won't, Mr. Caudle; you'll not serve me that trick again; for I've locked the door, and hid the key. There's no getting hold of you all the day-time—but here you can't leave me. You needn't groan again, Mr. Caudle.

"Now, Caudle, dear, do let us talk comfortably. After all, love, there's a good many folks, who, I dare say, don't get on half so well as we've done. We've both our little tempers, perhaps; but you *are* aggravating; you must own that, Caudle. Well, never mind; we won't talk of it; I won't scold you now. We'll talk of next Sunday, love. We never have kept our wedding-day, and I think it would be a nice day to have our friends. What do you say? *They'd think it hypocrisy?* No hypocrisy at all. I'm sure I try to be comfortable; and if ever man was happy, *you* ought to be. No, Caudle, no; it isn't nonsense to keep wedding-days; it isn't a deception on the world; and if it is, how many people do it? I'm sure, it's only a proper compliment that a man owes to his wife. Look at the Winkles—don't they give a dinner every year? Well, I know, and if they do fight a little in the course of the twelvemonth, that's nothing to do with it. They keep their wedding-day, and their acquaintance have nothing to do with anything else.

"As I say, Caudle, it's only a proper compliment that a man owes to his wife to keep his wedding-day. It's as much as to say to the whole world—'There! if I had to marry again, my blessed wife's the only woman I'd choose!' Well! I see nothing to groan at, Mr. Caudle— no, nor to sigh at either; but I know what you mean: I'm sure, what would have become of you, if you hadn't married as you have done—why, you'd have been a lost creature! I know it; I know your habits, Caudle; and—I don't like to say it—but you'd have been little better than a ragamuffin. Nice scrapes you'd have got into, I know, if you hadn't had me for a wife. The trouble I've had to keep you respectable—and what's my thanks? Ha! I only wish you had some women!

"But we won't quarrel, Caudle. No; you don't mean anything, I know. We'll have this little dinner, eh? Just a few friends? Now don't say you don't care—that isn't the way to speak to a wife! and especially the wife I've been to you, Caudle. Well, you agree to the dinner, eh? Now don't grunt, Mr. Caudle, but speak out. You'll keep your wedding-day? What! *If I'll let you go to sleep?* Ha! that's unmanly, Caudle; can't you say 'Yes' without anything else? I say—can't you say 'Yes?'—There, bless you! I knew you would.

"And now, Caudle, what shall we have for dinner? No—we won't talk of it to-morrow; we'll talk of it now, and then it will be off my mind. I should like something particular—something out of the way—just to show that we thought the day something. I should like—Mr. Caudle, you're not asleep? *What do I want?* Why you know I want to settle about the dinner. *Have what I like?* No: as it's your fancy to keep the day, it's only right that I should try to please you. We never had one, Caudle; so what do you think of a haunch of venison? What do you say? *Mutton will do?* Ha! that shows what you think of your wife: I dare say if it was with any of your club friends—any of your pot-house companions—you'd have no objection to venison. I say if— what do you mutter? *Let it be venison?* Very well. And now about the fish? What do you think of a nice turbot? No, Mr. Caudle, brill won't do—it shall be turbot, or there shan't be any fish at all. Oh, what a mean man you are, Caudle! Shall it be turbot? *It shall?* Very well. And now about the soup—now, Caudle, don't swear at the soup in that manner; you know there must be soup. Well, once in a way, and just to show our friends how happy we've been, we'll have some real turtle. *No, you won't, you'll have nothing but mock?* Then, Mr. Caudle, you may sit at the table by yourself. Mock-turtle on a wedding-day! Was there ever such an insult? What do you say? *Let it be real then, for once?* Ha, Caudle, as I say, you were a very different person fourteen years ago.

"And Caudle, you'll look after the venison? There's a place I know, somewhere in the City, where you get it beautiful. You'll look to it? *You will?* Very well.

"And now who shall we invite? *Who I like?* Now, you know, Caudle, that's nonsense; because I only like whom you like. I suppose the Prettymans must come? But understand, Caudle, I don't have Miss Prettyman: I'm not going to have my peace of mind destroyed under my own roof: if she comes, I don't appear at the table. What do you say? *Very well?* Very well be it, then.

"And now, Caudle, you'll not forget the venison? In the City, my dear? You'll not forget the venison? A haunch, you know: a nice haunch. And you'll not forget the venison?—"

"Three times did I fall off to sleep," says Caudle, "and three times did my wife nudge me with her elbow, exclaiming—'You'll not forget the venison?' At last I got into a sound slumber, and dreamt I was a pot of currant jelly."

Lecture XX

"Brother" Caudle Has Been to a Masonic Charitable Dinner. Mrs. Caudle Has Hidden the "Brother's" Cheque-Book

"All I say is this: I only wish I'd been born a man. What do you say? *You wish I had?* Mr. Caudle, I'll not lie quiet in my own bed to be insulted. Oh, yes, you *did* mean to insult me. I know what you mean. You mean, if I *had* been born a man, you'd never have married me. That's a pretty sentiment, I think? and after the wife I've been to you. And now I suppose you'll be going to public dinners every day! it's no use your telling me you've only been to one before; that's nothing to do with it—nothing at all. Of course you'll be out every night now. I knew what it would come to when you were made a mason: when you were once made a 'brother', as you call yourself, I knew where the husband and father would be;—I'm sure, Caudle, and though I'm your own wife, I grieve to say it—I'm sure you haven't so much heart, that you have any to spare for people out of doors. Indeed, I should like to see the man who has! No, no, Caudle; I'm by no means a selfish woman—quite the contrary; I love my fellow-creatures as a wife and mother of a family, who has only to look to her own husband and children, ought to love 'em.

"A 'brother', indeed! What would you say, if I was to go and be made a 'sister'? Why, I know very well—the house wouldn't hold you.

"*Where's your watch?* How should I know where your watch is? You ought to know. But to be sure, people who go to public dinners never know where anything is when they come home. You've lost it no doubt; and 'twill serve you quite right if you have. If it should be gone—and nothing more likely—I wonder if any of your 'brothers' will give you another? Catch 'em doing it.

"*You must find your watch? And you'll get up for it?* Nonsense—don't be foolish—lie still. Your watch is on the mantelpiece. Ha! isn't it a good thing for you, you've somebody to take care of it?

"What do you say? *I'm a dear creature?* Very dear, indeed, you think me, I dare say. But the fact is, you don't know what you're talking about to-night. I'm a fool to open my lips to you—but I can't help it.

"*Where's your watch?* Haven't I told you—on the mantelpiece. *All right, indeed?* Pretty conduct you men call all right. There, now, hold your tongue, Mr. Caudle, and go to sleep: I'm sure 'tis the best thing you can do to-night. You'll be able to listen to reason to-morrow morning; now, it's thrown away upon you.

"*Where's your cheque-book?* Never mind your cheque-book. I took care of that. *What business had I to take it out of your pocket?* Every business. No, no. If you choose to go to public dinners, why—as I'm only your wife—I can't help it. But I know what fools men are made of there; and if I know it, you never take your cheque-book again with you. What! Didn't I see your name down last year for ten pounds? 'Job Caudle, Esq., 10*l*.' It looked very well in the newspapers, of course: and you thought yourself a somebody, when they knocked the tavern tables; but I only wish I'd been there—yes, I only wish I'd been in the gallery. If I wouldn't have told a piece of my mind, I'm not alive. Ten pounds, indeed! and the world thinks you a very fine person for it. I only wish I could bring the world here, and show 'em what's wanted at home. I think the world would alter their mind then; yes—a little.

"What do you say? *A wife has no right to pick her husband's pocket?* A pretty husband you are to talk in that way. Never mind: you can't prosecute her for it— or I've no doubt you would; none at all. Some men would do anything. What? *You've a bit of a head-ache?* I hope you have—and a good bit, too. You've been to the right place for it. No—I won't hold my tongue. It's all very well for you men to go to taverns—and talk—and toast—and hurra—and—I wonder you're not all ashamed of yourselves to drink the Queen's health with all the honours, I believe, you call it—yes, pretty honours, you pay to the sex—I say, I wonder you're not ashamed to drink that blessed creature's health, when you've only to think how you use your own wives at home. But the hypocrites that the men are—oh!

"*Where's your watch?* Haven't I told you? It's under your pillow—there, you needn't be feeling for it. I tell you it's under your pillow. *It's all right?* Yes; a great deal you know of what's right just now. Ha! was there ever any poor soul used as I am! *I'm a dear creature?* Pah! Mr. Caudle! I've only to say, I'm tired of your conduct— quite tired, and don't care how soon there's an end of it.

"*Why did I take your cheque-book?* I've told you—to save you from ruin, Mr. Caudle. *You're not going to be ruined?* Ha! you don't know anything when you're out! I know what they do at those public dinners—charities, they call 'em; pretty charities! True Charity, I believe, always dines at home. I know what they do: the whole system's a trick. No: *I'm not a stony-hearted creature*: and you ought to be ashamed to say so of your wife and the mother of your children—but, you'll not make me cry to-night, I can tell you—I was going to say that— oh! you're such an aggravating man I don't know what I was going to say!

"*Thank Heaven?* What for! I don't see that there's anything to thank Heaven about! I was going to say, I know the trick of public dinners. They get a lord or a duke, if they can catch him—anything to make people say they've dined with nobility, that's it—yes, they get one of these people with a star perhaps in his coat, to take the chair—and to talk all sorts of sugarplum things about charity—and to make foolish men, with wine in 'em, feel that they've no end of money; and then— shutting their eyes to their wives and families at home —all the while that their own faces are red and flushed like poppies, and they think to-morrow will never come —and they get 'em to put their hand to paper. Then they make 'em pull out their cheques. But I took your book, Mr. Caudle—you couldn't do it a second time. What are you laughing at? *Nothing?* It's no matter: I shall see it in the paper to-morrow; for if you gave anything, you were too proud to hide it. I know *your* charity.

"*Where's your watch?* Haven't I told you fifty times where it is? In the pocket—over your head—of course. Can't you hear it tick? No: you can hear nothing to-night.

"And now, Mr. Caudle, I should like to know whose hat it is you've brought home? You went out with a beaver worth three-and-twenty shillings—the second time you've worn it—and you bring home a thing that no Jew in his senses would give me fivepence for. I couldn't even get a pot of primroses—and you know I always turn your old hats into roots—not a pot of primroses for it. I'm certain of it now—I've often thought it—but now I'm sure that some people dine out only to change their hats.

"*Where's your watch?* Caudle, you're bringing me to an early grave!"

We hope that Caudle was penitent for his conduct; indeed, there is, we think, evidence that he was so: for to this lecture he has appended no comment. The man had not the face to do it.

MR. CAUDLE BRINGS HOME THE WRONG HAT.

Lecture XXI

Mr. Caudle Has Not Acted "Like a Husband" at the Wedding Dinner

"Ah me! It's no use wishing—none at all: but I do wish that yesterday fourteen years could come back again. Little did I think, Mr. Caudle, when you brought me home from church, your lawful wedded wife—little, I say, did I think that I should keep my wedding dinner in the manner I have done to-day. Fourteen years ago! Yes, I see you now in your blue coat, with bright buttons, and your white watered-satin waistcoat, and a moss rosebud in your button-hole, which you said was like me. What? *You never talked such nonsense?* Ha! Mr. Caudle, you don't know what you talked that day—but I do. Yes; and you then sat at the table as if your face, as I may say, was buttered with happiness, and—What? No. Mr. Caudle, don't say that; *I* have not wiped the butter off—not I. If you above all men are not happy, you ought to be, gracious knows!

"Yes, I *will* talk of fourteen years ago. Ha! you sat beside me then, and picked out all sorts of nice things for me. You'd have given me pearls and diamonds to eat if I could have swallowed 'em. Yes, I say, you sat beside me, and—What do you talk about? *You couldn't sit beside me to-day?* That's nothing at all to do with it. But it's so like you. I can't speak but you fly off to something else.

Ha! and when the health of the young couple was drunk, what a speech you made then! It was delicious! How you made everybody cry, as if their hearts were breaking; and I recollect it as if it was yesterday, how the tears ran down dear father's nose, and how dear mother nearly went into a fit! Dear souls! They little thought, *with all your* fine talk, how you'd use me! *How have you used me?* Oh, Mr. Caudle, how can you ask that question? It's well for you I can't see you blush. *How* have you used me?

"Well, that the same tongue could make a speech like that, and then talk as it did to-day! *How did you talk!* Why shamefully! What did you say about your wedded happiness? Why, nothing. What did you say about your wife? Worse than nothing: just as if she were a bargain you were sorry for, but were obliged to make the best of. What do you say? *And bad's the best?* If you say that again, Caudle, I'll rise from my bed. *You didn't say it?* What, then, did you say? Something very like it, I know. Yes, a pretty speech of thanks for a husband! And everybody could see that you didn't care a pin for me; and that's why you had 'em here: that's why you invited 'em, to insult me to their faces. What? *I made you invite then?* Oh, Caudle, what an aggravating man you are!

"I suppose you'll say next I made you invite Miss Prettyman? Oh yes; don't tell me that her brother brought her without your knowing it? What? *Didn't I hear him say so?* Of course I did; but do you suppose I'm quite a fool? Do you think I don't know that that was all settled between you? And she must be a nice person to come unasked to a woman's house? But I know why she came. Oh yes; she came to look about her. *What do I mean?* Oh, the meaning's plain enough. She came to see

MR. CAUDLE AND MISS PRETTYMAN.

how she should like the rooms—how she should like my seat at the fireplace; how she—and if it isn't enough to break a mother's heart to be treated so!—how she should like my dear children.

"Now, it's no use your bouncing about at—but of course that's it; I can't mention Miss Prettyman, but you fling about as if you were in a fit. Of course that shows there's something in it. Otherwise, why should you disturb yourself? Do you think I didn't see her looking at the cyphers on the spoons as if she already saw mine scratched out and hers there? No, I shan't drive you mad, Mr. Caudle; and if I do it's your own fault. No other man would treat the wife of his bosom in—what do you say? *You might as well have married a hedgehog?* Well, now it's come to something! But it's always the case! Whenever you've seen that Miss Prettyman, I'm sure to be abused. A hedgehog! A pretty thing for a woman to be called by her husband! Now you don't think I'll lie quietly in bed, and be called a

117

hedgehog—do you, Mr. Caudle?

"Well, I only hope Miss Prettyman had a good dinner, that's all. *I* had none! You know I had none—how was I to get any? You know that the only part of the turkey I care for is the merrythought. And that, of course, went to Miss Prettyman. Oh, I saw you laugh when you put it on her plate! And you don't suppose, after such an insult as that, I'd taste another thing upon the table? No, I should hope I have more spirit than that. Yes; and you took wine with her four times. What do you say? *Only twice?* Oh, you were so lost—fascinated, Mr. Caudle; yes, fascinated—that you didn't know what you did. However, I do think while I'm alive I might be treated with respect at my own table. I say, while I'm alive; for I know I shan't last long, and then Miss Prettyman may come and take it all. I'm wasting daily, and no wonder. I never say anything about it, but every week my gowns are taken in.

"I've lived to learn something, to be sure! Miss Prettyman turned up her nose at my custards. It isn't sufficient that you're always finding fault yourself, but you must bring women home to sneer at me at my own table. What do you say? *She didn't turn up her nose?* I know she did; not but what it's needless—Providence has turned it up quite enough for her already. And she must give herself airs over my custards! Oh, I saw her mincing with the spoon as if she was chewing sand. What do you say? *She praised my plum-pudding?* Who asked her to praise it? Like her impudence, I think!

"Yes, a pretty day I've passed. I shall not forget this wedding-day, I think! And as I say, a pretty speech you made in the way of thanks. No, Caudle, if I was to live a hundred years—you needn't groan, Mr. Caudle, I shall not trouble you half that time—if I was to live a hundred years, I should never forget it. Never! You didn't even so much as bring one of your children into your speech. And—dear creatures!—what have *they* done to offend you? No; I shall not drive you mad. It's you, Mr. Caudle, who'll drive me mad. Everybody says so.

"And you suppose I didn't see how it was managed, that you and *that* Miss Prettyman were always partners at whist! *How was it managed*? Why, plain enough. Of course you packed the cards, and could cut what you liked. You'd settled that, between you. Yes; and when she took a trick, instead of leading off a trump—*she* play whist, indeed!—what did you say to her, when she found it was wrong? Oh—It was impossible that *her* heart should mistake! And this, Mr. Caudle, before people—with your own wife in the room!

"And Miss Prettyman—I won't hold my tongue. I *will* talk of Miss Prettyman: who's she, indeed, that I shouldn't talk of her? I suppose she thinks she sings? What do you say? *She sings like a mermaid*? Yes, very—very like a mermaid: for she never sings but she exposes herself. She might, I think, have chosen another song. '*I love somebody*', indeed; as if I didn't know who was meant by that 'somebody'; and all the room knew it, of course; and that was what it was done for, nothing else.

"However, Mr. Caudle, as my mind's made up, I shall say no more about the matter to-night, but try to go to sleep."

"And to my astonishment and gratitude," writes Caudle, "she kept her word."

Lecture XXII

Caudle Comes Home in the Evening, as Mrs. Caudle Has "Just Stepped Out, Shopping". On her Return, at Ten, Caudle Remonstrates

"You ought to have had a slave—yes, a black slave, and not a wife. I'm sure, I'd better been born a Negro at once—much better. *What's the matter, now?* Well, I like that. Upon my life, Mr. Caudle, that's very cool. I can't leave the house just to buy a yard of riband, but you storm enough to carry the roof off. *You didn't storm?— you only spoke?* Spoke, indeed! No, sir: I've not such superfine feelings; and I don't cry out before I'm hurt. But you ought to have married a woman of stone, for you feel for nobody: that is, for nobody in your own house. I only wish you'd show some of your humanity at home, if ever so little—that's all.

"What do you say? *Where's my feelings, to go a shopping at night?* When would you have me go? In the broiling sun, making my face like a gipsy's? I don't see anything to laugh at, Mr. Caudle; but you think of anybody's face before your wife's. Oh, that's plain enough; and all the world can see it. I dare say, now, if it was Miss Prettyman's face—now, now, Mr. Caudle! What are you throwing yourself about for? I suppose Miss Prettyman isn't so wonderful a person that she isn't to be named? I suppose she's flesh and blood. What? *You don't know?* Ha! I don't know that.

121

"What, Mr. Caudle? *You'll have a separate room?—you'll not be tormented in this manner?* No, you won't, sir—not while I'm alive. A separate room! And you call yourself a religious man, Mr. Caudle. I'd advise you to take down the Prayer Book, and read over the Marriage Service. A separate room, indeed! Caudle, you're getting quite a heathen. A separate room! Well, the servants would talk then! But no: no man—not the best that ever trod, Caudle—should ever make me look so contemptible.

"I *shan't* go to sleep; and you ought to know me better than to ask me to hold my tongue. Because you come home when I've just stepped out to do a little shopping, you're worse than a fury. I should like to know how many hours I sit up for you? What do you say? *Nobody wants me to sit up?* Ha! that's like the gratitude of men—just like 'em! But a poor woman can't leave the house, that—what! *Why can't I go at reasonable hours?* Reasonable! What do you call eight o'clock? If I went out at eleven and twelve, as you come home, then you might talk; but seven or eight o'clock—why it's the cool of the evening; the nicest time to enjoy a walk; and, as I say, do a little bit of shopping. Oh yes, Mr. Caudle, I do think of the people that are kept in the shops just as much as you; but that's nothing at all to do with it. I know what you'd have. You'd have all those young men let away early from the counter to improve what you please to call their minds. Pretty notions you pick up among a set of free-thinkers, and I don't know what! When I was a girl, people never talked of minds—intellect, I believe you call it. Nonsense! a new-fangled thing, just come up; and the sooner it goes out, the better.

"WHY CAN'T I GO AT REASONABLE HOURS?"

"Don't tell me! What are shops for if they're not to be open late and early too? And what are shopmen, if they're not always to attend upon their customers? People pay for what they have, I suppose; and ar'n't to be told when they shall come and lay their money out, and when they shan't? Thank goodness! if one shop shuts, another keeps open; and I always think it a duty I owe to myself to go to the shop that's open last: it's the only way to punish the shopkeepers that are idle, and give themselves airs about early hours.

123

"Besides, there's some things I like to buy best at candlelight. Oh, don't talk to me about humanity! Humanity, indeed, for a pack of tall, strapping young fellows—some of 'em big enough to be shown for giants! And what have they to do? Why nothing, but to stand behind a counter, and talk civility. Yes, I know your notions; you say that everybody works too much: I know that. You'd have all the world do nothing half its time but twiddle its thumbs, or walk in the parks, or go to picture-galleries, and museums, and such nonsense. Very fine, indeed; but, thank goodness! the world isn't come to that pass yet.

"What do you say I am, Mr. Caudle? *A foolish woman, that can't look beyond my own fireside?* Oh yes, I can; quite as far as you, and a great deal farther. But I can't go out shopping a little with my dear friend, Mrs. Wittles—what do you laugh at? Oh, don't they? Don't women know what friendship is? Upon my life you've a nice opinion of us! Oh, yes, we *can*—we can look outside of our own fenders, Mr. Caudle. And if we can't, it's all the better for our families. A blessed thing it would be for their wives and children if men couldn't either. You wouldn't have lent that five pounds—and I dare say a good many other five pounds that I know nothing of—if you—a lord of the creation!—had half the sense women have. You seldom catch us, I believe, lending five pounds. I should think not.

"No: we won't talk of it to-morrow morning. You're not going to wound my feelings when I come home, and think I'm to say nothing about it. You have called me an inhuman person; you have said I have no thought, no feeling for the health and comfort of my fellow creatures; I don't know what you haven't called me; and

124

only for buying a—but I shan't tell you what; no, I won't satisfy you there—but you've abused me in this manner, and only for shopping up to ten o'clock. You've a great deal of fine compassion, you have! I'm sure the young man that served me could have knocked down an ox; yes, strong enough to lift a house: but you can pity him—oh yes, you can be all kindness for him, and for the world, as you call it. Oh, Caudle, what a hypocrite you are! I only wish the world knew how you treated your poor wife.

"What do you say? *For the love of mercy let you sleep?* Mercy, indeed! I wish you could show a little of it to other people. Oh yes, I *do* know what mercy means; but that's no reason I should go shopping a bit earlier than I do—and I won't—No; you've preached this over to me again and again; you've made me go to meetings to hear all about it: but that's no reason women shouldn't shop just as late as they choose. It's all very fine, as I say, for you men to talk to us at meetings, where, of course, we smile and all that—and sometimes shake our white pocket-handkerchiefs—and where you say we have the power of early hours in our own hands. To be sure we have; and we mean to keep it. That is, I do. You'll never catch me shopping till the very last thing; and—as a matter of principle—I'll always go to the shop that keeps open latest. It does the young men good to keep 'em close to business. Improve their minds, indeed! Let 'em out at seven, and they'd improve nothing but their billiards. Besides, if they want to improve themselves, can't they get up, this fine weather, at three? Where there's a will, there's a way, Mr. Caudle."

"I thought," writes Caudle, "that she had gone to

sleep. In this hope, I was dozing off when she jogged me, and thus declared herself:—'Caudle, you want nightcaps; but see if I budge to buy 'em till nine at night!'"

Mrs. Caudle "Wishes to Know if They're Going to the Sea-Side, or Not, this Summer—That's All"

"Hot? Yes, it *is* hot. I'm sure one might as well be in an oven as in town this weather. You seem to forget it's July, Mr. Caudle. I've been waiting quietly—have never spoken; yet, not a word have you said of the sea-side yet. Not that I care for it myself—oh, no; my health isn't of the slightest consequence. And, indeed, I was going to say—but I won't—that the sooner, perhaps, I'm out of this world, the better. Oh, yes: I dare say you think so— of course you do, else you wouldn't lie there saying nothing. You're enough to aggravate a saint, Caudle; but you shan't vex me. No! I've made up my mind, and never intend to let you vex me again. Why should I worry myself?

"But all I want to ask you is this: do you intend to go to the sea-side this summer? *Yes? you'll go to Gravesend?* Then you'll go alone, that's all I know. Gravesend! You might as well empty a salt-cellar in the New River, and call that the sea-side. What? *It's handy for business?* There you are again! I can never speak of taking a little enjoyment, but you fling business in my teeth. I'm sure you never let business stand in the way of your own pleasure, Mr. Caudle—not you. It would be all the better for your family if you did.

"You know that Matilda wants sea-bathing; you know it, or ought to know it, by the looks of the child; and yet—I know you, Caudle—you'd have let the summer pass over, and never said a word about the matter. What do you say? *Margate's so expensive?* Not at all. I'm sure it will be cheaper for us in the end; for if we don't go, we shall all be ill—every one of us—in the winter. Not that my health is of any consequence: I know that well enough. It never was yet. You know Margate's the only place I can eat a breakfast at, and yet you talk of Gravesend! But what's my eating to you? You wouldn't care if I never eat at all. You never watch my appetite like any other husband, otherwise you'd have seen what it's come to.

"What do you say? *How much will it cost?* There you are, Mr. Caudle, with your meanness again. When you want to go yourself to Blackwall or to Greenwich, you never ask, how much will it cost? What? *You never go to Blackwall?* Ha! I don't know that; and if you don't, that's nothing at all to do with it. Yes, you can give a guinea a plate for whitebait for yourself. No, sir; I'm not a foolish woman: and I know very well what I'm talking about—nobody better. A guinea for whitebait for yourself, when you grudge a pint of shrimps for your poor family. Eh? *You don't grudge 'em anything?* Yes, it's very well for you to lie there and say so. *What will it cost?* It's no matter what it will cost, for we won't go at all now. No; we'll stay at home. We shall all be ill in the winter—every one of us, all but you; and nothing ever makes you ill. I've no doubt we shall all be laid up, and there'll be a doctor's bill as long as a railroad; but never mind that. It's better—much better—to pay for nasty physic than for fresh air and wholesome salt water.

Don't call me 'woman,' and ask 'what it will cost'. I tell you, if you were to lay the money down before me on that quilt, I wouldn't go now—certainly not. It's better we should all be sick; yes, then you'll be pleased.

"That's right, Mr. Caudle; go to sleep. It's like your unfeeling self! I'm talking of our all being laid up; and you, like any stone, turn round and begin to go to sleep. Well, I think that's a pretty insult! *How can you sleep with such a splinter in your flesh?* I suppose you mean to call me the splinter?—and after the wife I've been to you! But no, Mr. Caudle, you may call me what you please; you'll not make me cry now. No, no: I don't throw away my tears upon any such person now. What? *Don't?* Ha! that's your ingratitude! But none of you men deserve that any woman should love you. My poor heart!

"Everybody else can go out of town except us. Ha! if I'd only married Simmons—What? *Why didn't I?* Yes, that's all the thanks I get. *Who's Simmons?* Oh, you know very well who Simmons is. He'd have treated me a little better, I think. He *was* a gentleman. *You can't tell?* May be not; but I can. With such weather as this, to stay melting in London; and when the painters are coming in! *You won't have the painters in?* But you must; and if they once come in, I'm determined that none of us shall stir then. Painting in July, with a family in the house! We shall all be poisoned, of course; but what do you care for that?

"*Why can't I tell you what it will cost?* How can I or any woman tell exactly what it will cost? Of course lodgings—and at Margate, too—are a little dearer than living at your own house. *Pooh! You know that?* Well, if you did, Mr. Caudle, I suppose there's no treason in

129

naming it. Still, if you take 'em for two months, they're cheaper than for one. No, Mr. Caudle, I shall not be quite tired of it in one month. No: and it isn't true that I no sooner get out than I want to get home again. To be sure, I was tired of Margate three years ago, when you used to leave me to walk about the beach by myself, to be stared at through all sorts of telescopes. But you don't do that again, Mr. Caudle, I can tell you.

"*What will I do at Margate?* Why isn't there bathing, and picking up shells; and ar'n't there the packets, with the donkeys; and the last new novel—whatever it is, to read—for the only place where I really relish a book is at the sea-side. No, it isn't that I like salt with my reading, Mr. Caudle! I suppose you call that a joke? You

MR. AND MRS. CAUDLE AT THE SEA-SIDE.

might keep your jokes for the day-time, I think. But as I was saying—only you always will interrupt me—the ocean always seems to me to open the mind. I see nothing to laugh at; but you always laugh when I say anything. Sometimes at the sea-side—specially when the tide's down—I feel so happy: quite as if I could cry.

"When shall I get the things ready? For next Sunday? *What will it cost?* Oh, there—don't talk of it. No: we won't go. I shall send for the painters, to-morrow. What? *I can go and take the children, and you'll stay?* No, sir: you go with me, or I don't stir. I'm not going to be turned loose like a hen with her chickens, and nobody to protect me. So we'll go on Monday? Eh?

"*What will it cost?* What a man you are! Why, Caudle, I've been reckoning that, with buff slippers and all, we can't well do it under seventy pounds. No: I won't take away the slippers, and say fifty: it's seventy pounds, and no less. Of course, what's over will be so much saved. Caudle, what a man you are! Well, shall we go on Monday? What do you say—*You'll see?* There's a dear. Then, Monday."

"Anything for a chance of peace," writes Caudle. "I consented to the trip for I thought I might sleep better in a change of bed."

Mrs. Caudle Dwells on Caudle's "Cruel Neglect" of her on Board the "Red Rover". Mrs. Caudle so "Ill with the Sea", that they Put Up at the Dolphin, Herne Bay

"Caudle, have you looked under the bed? *What for?* Bless the man! Why, for thieves to be sure. Do you suppose I'd sleep in a strange bed, without? Don't tell me it's nonsense! I shouldn't sleep a wink all night. Not that you'd care for that: not that you'd—hush! I'm sure I hear somebody. No; it's not a bit like a mouse. Yes; that's like you—laugh. It would be no laughing matter if—I'm sure there *is* somebody!—I'm sure there is!

"——Yes, Mr. Caudle; now I *am* satisfied. Any other man would have got up and looked himself; especially after my sufferings on board that nasty ship. But catch you stirring! Oh, no! You'd let me lie here and be robbed and killed, for what you'd care. Why you're not going to sleep! What do you say? *It's the strange air— and you're always sleepy in a strange air?* That shows the feelings you have, after what I've gone through. And yawning, too, in that brutal manner! Caudle, you've no more heart than that wooden figure in a white petticoat at the front of the ship.

"No; I *couldn't* leave my temper at home. I dare say! Because for once in your life you've brought me out— yes, I say once, or two or three times, it isn't more; because, as I say, you once bring me out, I'm to be a slave and say nothing. Pleasure, indeed! A great deal of pleasure I'm to have, if I'm to hold my tongue. A nice way that of pleasing a woman.

"Dear me! if the bed doesn't spin round and dance about! I've got all that filthy ship in my head! No: I shan't be well in the morning. But nothing ever ails anybody but yourself. You needn't groan in that way, Mr. Caudle, disturbing the people, perhaps, in the next room. It's a mercy I'm alive, I'm sure. If once I wouldn't have given all the world for anybody to have thrown me overboard! What are you smacking your lips at, Mr. Caudle? But I know what you mean—of course, you'd never have stirred to stop 'em: not you. And then you might have known that the wind would have blown to-day; but that's why you came.

"Whatever I should have done if it hadn't been for that good soul—that blessed Captain Large! I'm sure all the women who go to Margate ought to pray for him; so attentive in sea-sickness, and so much of a gentleman! How I should have got down stairs without him when I first began to turn, I don't know. Don't tell me I never complained to you—you might have seen I was ill. And when everybody was looking like a bad wax-candle, you could walk about, and make what you call your jokes upon the little buoy that was never sick at the Nore, and such unfeeling trash.

"Yes, Caudle; we've now been married many years, but if we were to live together for a thousand years to come—what are you clasping your hands at?—a thousand years to come I say, I shall never forget your conduct this day. You could go to the other end of the ship and smoke a cigar, when you knew I should be ill—oh, you knew it; for I always am. The brutal way, too, in which you took that cold brandy-and-water—you thought I didn't see you; but ill as I was, hardly able to hold my head up, I was watching you all the time. Three glasses of cold brandy-and-water; and you sipped 'em, and drank the health of people you didn't care a pin about; whilst the health of your own lawful wife was nothing. Three glasses of brandy-and-water, and *I* left—as I may say—alone! You didn't hear 'em, but everybody was crying shame of you.

"What do you say? *A good deal my own fault? I took*

MR. CAUDLE ENJOYS HIS BRANDY-AND-WATER.

too much dinner? Well, you are a man! If I took more than the breast and leg of that young goose—a thing, I may say, just out of the shell—with the slightest bit of stuffing, I'm a wicked woman. What do you say? *Lobster salad?* La!—how can you speak of it? A month old baby would have eaten more. What? *Gooseberry pie?* Well, if you'll name that, you'll name anything. Ate too much indeed! Do you think I was going to pay for a dinner, and eat nothing? No, Mr. Caudle; it's a good thing for you that I know a little more of the value of money than that.

"But, of course, you were better engaged than in attending to me. Mr. Prettyman came on board at Gravesend. A planned thing, of course. You think I didn't see him give you a letter. *It wasn't a letter; it was a newspaper?* I dare say; ill as I was, I had my eyes. It was the smallest newspaper I ever saw, that's all. But of course, a letter from Miss Prettyman——Now, Caudle, if you begin to cry out in that manner, I'll get up. Do you forget that you're not at your own house? Making that noise! Disturbing everybody! Why we shall have the landlord up! And you could smoke and drink 'forward' as you call it. What? *You couldn't smoke anywhere else?* That's nothing to do with it. Yes; forward. What a pity that Miss Prettyman wasn't with you. I'm sure nothing could be too forward for her. No, I won't hold my tongue; and I ought not to be ashamed of myself. It isn't treason, is it, to speak of Miss Prettyman? After all I've suffered to-day, and I'm not to open my lips? Yes; I'm to be brought away from my own home, dragged down here to the sea-side, and made ill; and I'm not to speak. I should like to know what next.

"It's a mercy that some of the dear children were not drowned; not that their father would have cared, so long as he could have had his brandy and cigars. Peter was as near through one of the holes as—*It's no such thing?* It's very well for you to say so, but you know what an inquisitive boy he is, and how he likes to wander among steam-engines. No, I won't let you sleep. What a man you are! What? *I've said that before?* That's no matter; I'll say it again. Go to sleep, indeed! as if one could never have a little rational conversation. No, I shan't be too late for the Margate boat in the morning; I can wake up at what hour I like, and you ought to know that by this time.

"A miserable creature they must have thought me in the ladies' cabin, with nobody coming down to see how I was. *You came a dozen times?* No, Caudle, that won't do. I know better. You never came at all. Oh, no! cigars and brandy took all your attention. And when I was so ill, that I didn't know a single thing that was going on about me, and you never came. Every other woman's husband was there—ha! twenty times. And what must have been my feelings to hear 'em tapping at the door, and making all sorts of kind enquiries—something like husbands!—and I was left to be ill alone? Yes; and you want to get me into an argument. You want to know, if I was so ill that I knew nothing, how could I know that you didn't come to the cabin-door? That's just like your aggravating way; but I'm not to be caught in that manner, Caudle. No."

"It is very possible," writes Caudle, "that she talked two hours more; but, happily, the wind got suddenly up—the waves bellowed—and, soothed by the sweet lullaby (to say nothing of the Dolphin's brandy-and-water), I somehow sank to repose."

Lecture XXV

Mrs. Caudle, Wearied of Margate, Has "A Great Desire to See France"

"Ar'n't you tired, Caudle? *No?* Well, was there ever such a man! But nothing ever tires you. Of course, it's all very well for you: yes, you can read your newspapers and—what? *So can I?* And I wonder what would become of the children if I did! No; it's enough for their father to lose his precious time, talking about politics, and bishops, and lords, and a pack of people who wouldn't care a pin if we hadn't a roof to cover us—it's well enough for—no, Caudle, no: I'm not going to worry you; I never worried you yet, and it isn't likely I should begin now. But that's always the way with you—always. I'm sure we should be the happiest couple alive, only you do so like to have all the talk to yourself. We're out upon pleasure, and therefore let's be comfortable. Still, I must say it: when you like, you're an aggravating man, Caudle, and you know it.

"*What have you done now?* There, now; we won't talk of it. No; let's go to sleep: otherwise, we shall quarrel—I know we shall. What have you done, indeed! That I can't leave my home for a few days, but I must be insulted! Everybody upon the pier saw it. *Saw what?* How can you lie there in the bed and ask me? Saw what, indeed! Of course, it was a planned thing!—regularly

139

settled before you left London. Oh yes; I like your innocence, Mr. Caudle; not knowing what I'm talking about. It's a heart-breaking thing for a woman to say of her own husband; but you've been a wicked man to me. Yes: and all your tossing and tumbling about in the bed won't make it any better.

"Oh, it's easy enough to call a woman 'a dear soul'. I must be very dear, indeed to you, when you bring down Miss Prettyman to—there now; you needn't shout like a wild savage. Do you know that you're not in your own house—do you know that we're in lodgings? What do you suppose the people will think of us? You needn't call out in that manner, for they can hear every word that's said. What do you say? *Why don't I hold my tongue then?* To be sure; anything for an excuse with you. Anything to stop my mouth. Miss Prettyman's to follow you here and I'm to say nothing. I know she *has* followed you; and if you were to go before a magistrate, and take a shilling oath to the contrary, I wouldn't believe you. No, Caudle; I wouldn't.

"*Very well then?* Ha! what a heart you must have, to say 'very well'; and after the wife I've been to you. I'm to be brought from my own home—dragged down here to the sea-side—to be laughed at before the world— don't tell me! Do you think I didn't see how she looked at you—how she puckered up her farthing mouth— and—what? *Why did I kiss her, then?* What's that to do with it? Appearances are one thing, Mr. Caudle; and feelings are another. As if women can't kiss one another without meaning anything by it! And you—I could see you—looked as cold and as formal at her as—well, Caudle! I wouldn't be the hypocrite you are for the world!

"There, now; I've heard all that story. I dare say she did come down to join her brother. How very lucky, though, that you should be here! Ha! ha! how very lucky that—ugh! ugh! ugh! and with the cough I've got upon me—oh, you've a heart like a sea-side flint! Yes, that's right. That's just like your humanity. I can't catch a cold, but it must be my own fault—it must be my thin shoes. I dare say you'd like to see me in ploughman's boots; 'twould be no matter to you how I disfigured myself. Miss Prettyman's foot, now, would be another thing—no doubt.

"I thought when you would make me leave home—I thought we were coming here on pleasure: but it's always the way you embitter my life. The sooner that I'm out of the world, the better. What do you say? *Nothing*? But I know what you mean better than if you talked an hour. I only hope you'll get a better wife, that's all, Mr. Caudle. What? *You'd not try*? Wouldn't you? I know you. In six months you'd fill up my place; yes, and dreadfully my dear children would suffer for it.

"Caudle, if you roar in that way, the people will give us warning to-morrow. *Can't I be quiet then*? Yes—that's like your artfulness: anything to make me hold my tongue. But we won't quarrel. I'm sure if it depended upon me, we might be as happy as doves. I mean it—and you needn't groan when I say it. Good night, Caudle. What do you say *Bless me*! Well, you are a dear soul, Caudle; and if it wasn't for that Miss Prettyman—no, I'm not torturing you. I know very well what I'm doing, and I wouldn't torture you for the world; but you don't know what the feelings of a wife are, Caudle; you don't.

"Caudle—I say, Caudle. Just a word, dear. *Well*?

141

Now, why should you snap me up in that way. *You want to go to sleep?* So do I; but that's no reason you should speak to me in that manner. You know, dear, you once promised to take me to France. *You don't recollect it?* Yes—that's like you; you don't recollect many things you've promised me; but I do. There's a boat goes on Wednesday to Boulogne, and comes back the day afterwards. *What of it?* Why for that time we could leave the children with the girls, and go nicely. *Nonsense?* Of course: if I want anything it's always nonsense. Other men can take their wives half over the world; but you think it quite enough to bring me down here to this hole of a place, where I know every pebble on the beach like an old acquaintance—where there's nothing to be seen but the same machines—the same jetty—the same donkeys—the same everything. But then, I'd forgot; Margate has an attraction for you—Miss Prettyman's here. No; I'm not censorious, and I wouldn't backbite an angel; but the way in which that young woman walks the sands at all hours—there! there!—I've done: I can't open my lips about that creature but you always storm.

"You know that I always wanted to go to France; and you bring me down here only on purpose that I should see the French cliffs—just to tantalise me, and for nothing else. If I'd remained at home—and it was against my will I ever came here—I should never have thought of France; but—to have it staring in one's face all day, and not be allowed to go! it's worse than cruel, Mr. Caudle—it's brutal. Other people can take their wives to Paris; but you always keep me moped up at home. And what for? Why, that I may know nothing— yes; just on purpose to make me look little and for nothing else.

MR. AND MRS. CAUDLE TAKE A TRIP TO BOULOGNE.

"*Heaven bless the woman?* Ha! you've good reason to say that, Mr. Caudle; for I'm sure she's little blessed by you. She's been kept a prisoner all her life—has never gone anywhere—oh yes! that's your old excuse, talking of the children. I want to go to France, and I should like to know what the children have to do with it? They're not babies *now*—are they. But you've always thrown the children in my face. If Miss Prettyman—there now; do you hear what you've done—shouting in that manner? The other lodgers are knocking overhead: who do you think will have the face to look at 'em to-morrow morning? *I* shan't—breaking people's rest in that way!

"Well, Caudle—I declare it's getting daylight, and

what an obstinate man you are!—tell me, shall I go to France?"

"I forget," says Caudle, "my precise answer; but I think I gave her a very wide permission to go somewhere, whereupon, though not without remonstrance as to the place—she went to sleep."

Lecture XXVI

Mrs. Caudle's First Night in France—"Shameful Indifference" of Caudle at the Boulogne Custom House

"I suppose, Mr. Caudle, you call yourself a man? I'm sure such men should never have wives. If I could have thought it possible you'd have behaved as you have done—and I might, if I hadn't been a forgiving creature, for you've never been like anybody else—if I could only have thought it, you'd never have dragged me to foreign parts. Never! Well, I *did* say to myself, if he goes to France, perhaps he may catch a little politeness—but no: you began as Caudle, and as Caudle you'll end. I'm to be neglected through life, now. Oh yes! I've quite given up all thoughts of anything but wretchedness—I've made up my mind to misery, now. *You're glad of it?* Well, you must have a heart to say that. I declare to you, Caudle, as true as I'm an ill-used woman, if it wasn't for the dear children far away in blessed England—if it wasn't for them, I'd never go back with you. No: I'd leave you in this very place. Yes; I'd go into a convent; for a lady on board told me there was plenty of 'em here. I'd go and be a nun for the rest of my days, and—I see nothing to laugh at, Mr. Caudle; that you should be shaking the bed-things up and down in that way.—But you always laugh at people's feelings; I wish you'd only some yourself. I'd be a nun, or a Sister

145

of Charity. *Impossible?* Ha! Mr. Caudle, you don't know even now what I can be when my blood's up. You've trod upon the worm long enough; some day won't you be sorry for it?

"Now none of your profane cryings out! You needn't talk about Heaven in that way: I'm sure you're the last person who ought. What I say is this. Your conduct at the Custom House was shameful—cruel! And in a foreign land too! But you brought me here that I might be insulted; you'd no other reason for dragging me from England. Ha! let me once get home, Mr. Caudle, and you may wear your tongue out before you get me into outlandish places again. *What have you done?* There now; that's where you're so aggravating. You behave worse than any Turk to me—what? *You wish you were a Turk?* Well, I think that's a pretty wish before your lawful wife! Yes—a nice Turk you'd make, wouldn't you? Don't think it.

"*What have you done?* Well, it's a good thing I can't see you, for I'm sure you must blush. Done, indeed! Why, when the brutes searched my basket at the Custom House! *A regular thing, is it?* Then if you knew that, why did you bring me here? No man who respected his wife would. And you could stand by, and see that fellow with moustachios rummage my basket; and pull out my night-cap and rumple the borders, and—well! if you'd had the proper feelings of a husband, your blood would have boiled again. But no! There you stood looking as mild as butter at the man, and never said a word: not when he crumpled my night-cap—it went to my heart like a stab—crumpled it as if it was any duster. I dare say if it had been Miss Prettyman's night-cap—oh, I don't care about your groaning—if it had been her night-cap, her hair-brush, her curl-papers, you'd have said something then. Oh, anybody with the spirit of a man would have spoken out if the fellow had had a thousand swords at his side. Well, all I know is this: if I'd have married somebody I could name, he wouldn't have suffered me to be treated in that way, not he!

"Now, don't hope to go to sleep, Mr. Caudle, and think to silence me in that manner. I know your art, but it won't do. It wasn't enough that my basket was turned topsy-turvy, but before I knew it, they spun me into another room, and—*How could you help that?* You never tried to help it. No; although it was a foreign land, and I don't speak French—not but what I know a good deal more of it than some people who give themselves airs about it—though I don't speak their nasty gibberish, still you let them take me away, and never cared how I was ever to find you again. In a strange country too! But I've no doubt that that's what you wished: yes, you'd have been glad enough to have got rid of me in that cowardly manner. If I could only know your secret thoughts, Caudle, that's what you brought me here for, to lose me. And after the wife I've been to you!

"What are you crying out? *For mercy's sake?* Yes; a great deal you know about mercy! Else you'd never have suffered me to be twisted into that room. To be searched indeed! As if I'd anything smuggled about me. Well, I will say it; after the way in which I've been used, if you'd the proper feelings of a man, you wouldn't sleep again for six months. Well, I know there was nobody but women there; but that's nothing to do with it. I'm sure, if I'd been taken up for picking pockets, they couldn't have used me worse. To be treated so—

and 'specially by one's own sex!—it's *that* that aggravates me.

"And that's all you can say? *What could you do?* Why, break open the door; I'm sure you must have heard my voice; you shall never make me believe you couldn't hear that. Whenever I shall sew the strings on again, I can't tell. If they didn't turn me out like a ship in a storm, I'm a sinner! And you laughed! *You didn't laugh?* Don't tell me; you laugh when you don't know anything about it; but I do.

THE BRUTES SEARCHED MRS. CAUDLE'S BASKET AT THE
CUSTOM HOUSE.

"And a pretty place you have brought me to. A most respectable place I must say! Where the women walk about without any bonnets to their heads, and the fish-girls with their bare legs—well you don't catch me eating any fish while I'm here. *Why not?* Why not—do you think I'd encourage people of that sort?

"What do you say? *Good night?* It's no use your saying that—I can't go to sleep so soon as you can. Especially with a door that has such a lock as that to it. How do we know who may come in? What? *All the locks are bad in France?* The more shame for you to bring me to such a place, then. It only shows how you value me.

"Well, I dare say you are tired. *I* am! But then, see what I've gone through. Well, we won't quarrel in a barbarous country. We won't do that. Caudle, dear— what's the French for lace? I know it, only I forget it. The French for lace, love? What! *Dentelle?* Now, you're not deceiving me? *You never deceived me yet?* Oh! don't say that. There isn't a married man in this blessed world can put his hand upon his heart in bed, and say that. French for lace, dear? Say it again. *Dentelle?* Ha! Dentelle! Good night, dear. Dentelle! Den—telle."

"I afterwards," writes Caudle, "found out to my cost wherefore she enquired about lace. For she went out in the morning with the landlady to buy a veil, giving only four pounds for what she could have bought in England for forty shillings!"

Lecture XXVII

Mrs. Caudle Returns to her Native Land. "Unmanly Cruelty" of Caudle, Who Has Refused "To Smuggle a Few Things" for her

"There, it isn't often that I ask you to do anything for me, Mr. Caudle, goodness knows! and when I do, I'm always refused—of course. Oh yes! anybody but your own lawful wife. Every other husband aboard the boat could behave like a husband—but I was left to shift for myself. To be sure, that's nothing new; I always am. Every other man, worthy to be called a man, could smuggle a few things for his wife—but I might as well be alone in the world. Not one poor half-dozen of silk stockings could you put in your hat for me; and everybody else was rolled in lace, and I don't know what. Eh? What, Mr. Caudle? *What do I want with silk stockings?* Well—it's come to something now! There was a time, I believe, when I had a foot—yes, and an ankle, too: but when once a woman's married, she has nothing of the sort; of course. No: I'm *not* a cherub, Mr. Caudle; don't say that. I know very well what I am.

"I dare say now, you'd have been delighted to smuggle for Miss Prettyman? Silk stockings become her! *You wish Miss Prettyman was in the moon?* Not you, Mr. Caudle; that's only your art—your hypocrisy. A nice person too she'd be for the moon: it would be none the brighter for her being in it, I know. And when you saw the Custom House officers look at me, as though they were piercing me through, what was your conduct? Shameful. You twittered about, and fidgeted, and flushed up as if I really *was* a smuggler. *So I was?* What had that to do with it? It wasn't the part of a husband I think, to fidget in that way, and show it. *You couldn't help it?* Humph! And you call yourself a person of strong mind, I believe? One of the lords of the creation! Ha! ha! couldn't help it!

"But I may do all I can to save the money, and this is always my reward. Yes, Mr. Caudle, I shall save a great deal. *How much?* I shan't tell you: I know your meanness—you'd want to stop it out of the house allowance. No: it's nothing to you where I got the money from to buy so many things. The money was my own. Well, and if it was yours first, that's nothing to do with it. No; I hav'n't saved it out of the puddings. But it's always the woman who saves who's despised. It's only your fine lady-wives who're properly thought of. If I was to ruin you, Caudle, then you'd think something of me.

"I shan't go to sleep. It's very well for you who're no sooner in bed, than you're fast as a church; but I can't sleep in that way. It's my mind keeps me awake. And after all, I do feel so happy to-night, it's very hard I can't enjoy my thoughts. *No: I can't think in silence!* There's much enjoyment in that to be sure! I've no doubt now you could listen to Miss Prettyman—oh, I don't care, I will speak. It was a little more than odd, I think, that she should be on the jetty when the boat came in. Ha! she'd been looking for you all the morning with a telescope, I've no doubt—she's bold enough for anything. And then how she sneered and giggled when she saw me—and said 'how fat I'd got': like her impudence, I think. What! *Well she might?* But I know what she wanted; yes—she'd have liked to have had me searched. She laughed on purpose.

"I only wish I'd taken two of the dear girls with me. What things I could have stitched about 'em! No—I'm not ashamed of myself to make my innocent children smugglers: the more innocent they looked, the better; but there you are with what you call your principles again; as if it wasn't given to everybody by nature to smuggle. I'm sure of it—it's born with us. And nicely I've cheated 'em this day. Lace, and velvet, and silk stockings, and other things—to say nothing of the tumblers and decanters. No: I didn't look as if I wanted a direction, for fear somebody should break me. That's another of what you call your jokes; but you should keep 'em for those who like 'em. *I* don't.

"*What have I made after all?* I've told you—you shall never never know. Yes, I know you'd have been fined a hundred pounds if they'd searched me; but I never meant that they should. I dare say you wouldn't smuggle—oh no! you don't think it worth your while. You're quite a conjuror, you are, Caudle. Ha! ha! ha! *What am I laughing at?* Oh, you little know—such a clever creature! Ha! ha! Well, now I'll tell you. I knew what an unaccommodating animal you were, so I made you smuggle whether or nor. *How?* Why, when you were out at the *Café*, I got your great rough coat, and if I didn't stitch ten yards of best black velvet under the lining I'm a sinful woman! And to see how innocent you looked when the officers walked round and round you! It was a happy moment, Caudle, to see you.

"What do you call it? *A shameful trick—unworthy of a*

wife? I couldn't care much for you? As if I didn't prove that, by trusting you with ten yards of velvet. But I don't care what you say: I've saved everything—all but that beautiful English novel, that I've forgot the name of. And if they didn't take it out of my hand, and chopped it to bits like so much dog's-meat. *Served me right?* And when I so seldom buy a book! No: I don't see how it served me right. If you can buy the same book in France for four shillings that people here have the impudence to ask more than a guinea for—well, if they *do* steal it, that's their affair, not ours. As if there was anything in a book to steal!

"And now, Caudle, when are you going home? What? *Our time isn't up?* That's nothing to do with it. If we even lose a week's lodging—and we mayn't do that—we shall save it again in living. But you're such a man! Your home's the last place with you. I'm sure I don't get a wink of a night, thinking what may happen. Three fires last week; and any one might as well have been at our house as not. *No—they mightn't?* Well, you know what I mean—but you're such a man!

"I'm sure, too, we've had quite enough of this place. But there's no keeping you out of the libraries, Caudle. You're getting quite a gambler. And I don't think it's a nice example to set to your children, raffling as you do for French clocks and I don't know what. But that's not the worst; you never win anything. Oh, I forgot. Yes; a needle case, that under my nose you gave to Miss Prettyman. A nice thing for a married man to make presents; and to such a creature as that, too. A needle case! I wonder whenever she has a needle in *her* hand!

"I know I shall feel ill with anxiety if I stop here. Nobody left in the house but that Mrs. Closepeg. And she is such a stupid woman. It was only last night that I dreamt I saw our cat quite a skeleton, and the canary stiff on its back at the bottom of the cage. You know, Caudle, I'm never happy when I'm away from home; and yet you will stay here. No, home's my comfort; I never want to stir over the threshold, and you know it. If thieves were to break in, what could that Mrs. Closepeg do against 'em? And so, Caudle, you'll go home on Saturday? Our dear—dear home! On Saturday, Caudle?"

"A NEEDLE CASE, THAT UNDER MY NOSE YOU GAVE TO MISS PRETTYMAN."

"What I answered," says Caudle, "I forget; but I know that on the Saturday, we were once again shipped on board the *Red Rover*."

Lecture XXVIII

Mrs. Caudle Has Returned Home.—The House (of course) "Not Fit to Be Seen". Mr. Caudle, in Self-Defence, Takes a Book

"After all, Caudle, it is something to get into one's own bed again. I *shall* sleep to-night. What! *You're glad of it?* That's like your sneering; I know what you mean. Of course; I never can think of making myself comfortable, but you wound my feelings. If you cared for your own bed like any other man, you'd not have stayed out till this hour. Don't say that I drove you out of the house as soon as we came in it. I only just spoke about the dirt and the dust—but the fact is, you'd be happy in a pigsty! I thought I could have trusted that Mrs. Closepeg with untold gold; and did you only see the hearthrug? When we left home there was a tiger in it: I should like to know who could make out the tiger, now? Oh, it's very well for you to swear at the tiger, but swearing won't revive the rug again. Else you might swear.

"You could go out and make yourself comfortable at your club. You little know how many windows are broken. How many do you think? No: I shan't tell you to-morrow—you shall know now. I'm sure. Talking about getting health at Margate; all my health went away directly I went into the kitchen. There's dear mother's china bowl cracked in two places. I could have sat down and cried when I saw it: a bowl I can recollect

157

HOME! SWEET HOME!—MRS. CAUDLE'S RETURN.

when I was a child. Eh? *I should have locked it up then?*
Yes; that's your feeling for anything of mine. I only wish
it had been your punch-bowl; but, thank goodness! I
think that's chipped.

"Well, you haven't answered about the windows—
you can't guess how many? *You don't care?* Well, if
nobody caught cold but you, it would be little matter.
Six windows clean out, and three cracked! *You can't help
it?* I should like to know where the money's to come
from to mend 'em! They shan't be mended, that's all.
Then you'll see how respectable the house will look.
But I know very well what you think. Yes; you're glad of
it. You think that this will keep me at home—but I'll
never stir out again. Then you can go to the sea-side by
yourself; then, perhaps, you can be happy with Miss
Prettyman?—Now, Caudle, if you knock the pillow

with your fist in that way, I'll get up. It's very odd that I can't mention that person's name, but you begin to fight the bolster, and do I don't know what. There must be something in it, or you wouldn't kick about so. A guilty conscience needs no—but you know what I mean.

"She wasn't coming to town for a week; and then, of a sudden, she'd had a letter. I dare say she had. And then, as she said, it would be company for her to come with us. No doubt. She thought I should be ill again, and down in the cabin: but with all her art, she does not know the depth of me—quite. Not but what I was ill; though, like a brute, you wouldn't see it.

"What do you say? *Good night, love?* Yes: you can be very tender, I dare say—like all of your sex—to suit your own ends: but I can't go to sleep with my head full of the house. The fender in the parlour will never come to itself again. I haven't counted the knives yet, but I've made up my mind that half of 'em are lost. No: I don't always think the worst; no, and I don't make myself unhappy before the time; but of course, that's my thanks for caring about your property. If there ar'n't spiders in the curtains as big as nutmegs, I'm a wicked creature. Not a broom has the whole place seen since I've been away. But as soon as I get up, won't I rummage the house out, that's all. I hadn't the heart to look at my pickles; but for all I left the door locked; I'm sure the jars have been moved. Yes; you can swear at pickles when you're in bed; but nobody makes more noise about 'em when you want 'em.

"I only hope they've been to the wine-cellar: then you may know what my feelings are. That poor cat, too—What? *You hate cats?* Yes, poor thing! because she's my favourite—that's it. If that cat could only speak—What? *It isn't necessary?* I don't know what you mean, Mr. Caudle: but if that cat could only speak, she'd tell me how she's been cheated. Poor thing! I know where the money's gone to that I left for her milk —I know. Why what have you got there, Mr. Caudle? A book? What! *If you ar'n't allowed to sleep, you'll read?* Well, now it is come to something! If that isn't insulting a wife to bring a book to bed, I don't know what wedlock is. But you shan't read, Caudle; no you shan't; not while I've strength to get up and put out a candle.

"And that's like your feelings! You can think a great deal of trumpery books; yes, you can't think too much of the stuff that's put into print; but for what's real and true about you, why you've the heart of a stone. I should like to know what that book's about? What? *Milton's Paradise Lost?* I thought some rubbish of the sort— something to insult me. A nice book, I think, to read in bed; and a very respectable person he was who wrote it. *What do I know of him?* Much more than you think. A very pretty fellow, indeed, with his six wives. What? *He hadn't six—he'd only three?* That's nothing to do with it; but of course you'll take his part. Poor women! A nice time they had with him, I dare say! And I've no doubt, Mr. Caudle, you'd like to follow Mr. Milton's example: else you wouldn't read the stuff he wrote. But you don't use me as he treated the poor souls who married him. Poets, indeed! I'd make a law against any of 'em having wives except upon paper; for goodness help the dear creatures tied to them! Like innocent moths lured by a candle! Talking of candles, you don't know that the lamp in the passage is split to bits! I say you don't—do you hear me, Mr. Caudle? Won't you answer? Do you know where you are? What? *In the Garden of Eden?* Are you? Then you've no business there at this time of night."

"And saying this," writes Caudle, "she scrambled from the bed, and put out the light."

Mrs. Caudle Thinks "The Time Has Come to Have a Cottage out of Town"

"Caudle, you ought to have had something nice to-night; for you're not well, love—I know you're not. Ha! that's like you men—so headstrong! You will have it that nothing ails you; but I can tell, Caudle. The eye of a wife—and such a wife as I've been to you—can at once see whether a husband's well or not. You've been turning like tallow all the week; and what's more you eat nothing, now. It makes me melancholy to see you at a joint. I don't say anything at dinner before the children; but I don't feel the less. No, no; you're not very well; and you're not as strong as a horse. Don't deceive yourself—nothing of the sort. No, and you don't eat as much as ever: and if you do, you don't eat with a relish, I'm sure of that. You can't deceive me there.

"But I know what's killing you. It's the confinement; it's the bad air you breathe; it's the smoke of London. Oh yes, I know your old excuse: you never found the air bad before. Perhaps not. But as people grow older, and get on in trade—and, after all, we've nothing to complain of, Caudle—London air always disagrees with 'em. Delicate health comes with money: I'm sure of it. What a colour you had once, when you'd hardly a sixpence; and now, look at you!

"'Twould add thirty years to your life—and think what a blessing that would be to me; not that I shall live a tenth part of the time—thirty years, if you'd take a nice little house somewhere at Brixton. *You hate Brixton?* I must say it, Caudle, that's so like you: any place that's really genteel, you can't abide. Now Brixton and Balham Hill I think delightful. So select! There, nobody visits nobody, unless they're somebody. To say nothing of the delightful pews that make the churches so respectable!

"However, do as you like. If you won't go to Brixton, what do you say to Clapham Common? Oh, that's a very fine story! Never tell me! No; you wouldn't be left alone, a Robinson Crusoe with wife and children, because you're in the retail way. What! *The retired wholesales never visit the retired retails at Clapham?* Ha! that's only your old sneering at the world, Mr. Caudle; but I don't believe it. And after all, people should keep to their station, or what was this life made for? Suppose a tallow-merchant does keep himself above a tallow-chandler—I call it only a proper pride. What? *You call it the aristocracy of fat?* I don't know what you mean by aristocracy; but I suppose it's only another of your dictionary words, that's hardly worth the finding out.

"What do you say to Hornsey or Muswell Hill? Eh? *Too high?* What a man you are! Well then—Battersea? *Too low?* You're an aggravating creature, Caudle, you must own that! Hampstead, then? *Too cold?* Nonsense; it would brace you up like a drum, Caudle; and that's what you want. But you don't deserve anybody to think of your health or your comforts either. There's some pretty spots, I'm told, about Fulham. Now, Caudle, I won't have you say a word against Fulham. That must be a sweet place: dry, and healthy, and every comfort of life about it—else is it likely that a bishop would live there? Now, Caudle, none of your heathen principles—I won't hear 'em. I think what satisfies a bishop ought to content you; but the politics you learn at that club are dreadful. To hear you talk of bishops—well, I only hope nothing will happen to you, for the sake of the dear children!

"A nice little house and a garden! I know it—I was born for a garden! There's something about it makes one feel so innocent. My heart somehow always opens and shuts at roses. And then what nice currant wine we could make! And again, get 'em as fresh as you will, there's no radishes like your own radishes! They're ten times as sweet! What? *And twenty times as dear?* Yes; there you go! Anything that I fancy, you always bring up the expense.

"No, Mr. Caudle, I should not be tired of it in a month. I tell you I was made for the country. But here you've kept me—and much you've cared about my health—here, you've kept me in this filthy London, that I hardly know what grass is made of. Much you care for your wife and family to keep 'em here to be all smoked like bacon. I can see it—it's stopping the children's growth; they'll be dwarfs, and have their father to thank for it. If you'd the heart of a parent, you couldn't bear to look at their white faces. Dear little Dick! he makes no breakfast. What? *He ate six slices this morning?* A pretty father you must be to count 'em. But that's nothing to what the dear child could do, if, like other children, he'd a fair chance.

"Ha! and when we could be so comfortable! But it's always the case, you never will be comfortable with me.

How nice and fresh you'd come up to business every morning; and what pleasure it would be for me to put a tulip or a pink in your button-hole, just, as I may say, to ticket you from the country.

"But, then, Caudle, you never were like any other man! But I know why you won't leave London. Yes, I know. Then, you think, you couldn't go to your filthy club—that's it. Then you'd be obliged to be at home, like any other decent man. Whereas, you might, if you liked, enjoy yourself under your own apple-tree, and I'm sure I should never say anything about your tobacco out of doors. My only wish is to make you happy, Caudle, and you won't let me do it.

"You don't speak love? Shall I look about a house tomorrow; It will be a broken day with me, for I'm going out to have little pet's ears bored—What? *You won't*

MRS. CAUDLE'S MORNING DECORATION.

have her ears bored? And why not, I should like to know? *It's a barbarous savage custom?* Oh, Mr. Caudle! the sooner you go away from the world, and live in a cave, the better. You're getting not fit for Christian society. What next? My ears were bored and—what? *So are yours?* I know what you mean—but that's nothing to do with it. My ears, I say, were bored, and so were dear mother's, and grandmother's before her; and I suppose there were no more savages in our family than in yours, Mr. Caudle? Besides—why should little pet's ears go naked any more than any of her sisters'? They wear ear-rings, you never objected before. What? *You've learned better now?* Yes, that's all with your filthy politics again. You'd shake all the world up in a dice-box, if you had your way: not that you care a pin about the world, only you'd like to get a better throw for yourself—that's all. But little pet *shall* be bored, and don't think to prevent it.

"I suppose she's to be married some day, as well as her sisters? And who'll look at a girl without ear-rings, I should like to know? If you knew any thing of the world, you'd know what a nice diamond ear-ring will some-times do—when one can get it—before this. But I know why you can't abide ear-rings now; Miss Prettyman doesn't wear 'em; she would—I've no doubt—if she could only get 'em. Yes—it's Miss Prettyman, who—

"There, Caudle, now be quiet, and I'll say no more about pet's ears at present. We'll talk when you're reasonable. I don't want to put you out of temper, goodness knows! And so, love, about the cottage? What? *'Twill be so far from business?* But it needn't be far, dearest. Quite a nice distance; so that on your late nights, you may always be at home, have your supper, get to bed, and all by eleven. Eh—sweet one?"

"I don't know what I answered," says Caudle, "but I know this; in less than a fortnight I found myself in a sort of a green bird-cage of a house, which my wife—gentle satirist—insisted upon calling 'The Turtle-Dovery'."

Mrs. Caudle Complains of the "Turtle-Dovery". Discovers Black-Beetles. —Thinks It "Nothing But Right" that Caudle Should Set up a Chaise

"You'd never have got me into this wilderness of a place, Mr. Caudle, if I'd only have thought what it was. Yes, that's right: throw it in my teeth that it was my choice—that's manly, isn't it? When I saw the place the sun was out, and it looked beautiful—now, it's quite another thing. No, Mr. Caudle; I don't expect you to command the sun—and if you talk about Joshua in that infidel way, I'll leave the bed. No, sir; I don't expect the sun to be in your power, but that's nothing to do with it. I talk about one thing, and you always start another. But that's your art.

"I'm sure a woman might as well be buried alive as live here. In fact, I am buried alive; I feel it. I stood at the window three hours this blessed day, and saw nothing but the postman. No: it isn't a pity that I hadn't something better to do; I had plenty; but that's my business, Mr. Caudle. I suppose I'm to be mistress of my own house? If not, I'd better leave it.

"And the very first night we were here, you know it, the black-beetles came into the kitchen. If the place didn't seem spread all over with a black cloth, I'm a story-teller. What are you coughing at, Mr. Caudle? I see nothing to cough at. But that's just your way of sneering. Millions of black-beetles! And as the clock strikes eight, out they march. What? *They're very punctual?* I know that. I only wish other people were half as punctual: 'twould save other people's money and other people's peace of mind. You know I hate a black-beetle! No: I don't hate so many things. But I do hate black-beetles, as I hate ill-treatment, Mr. Caudle. And now I have enough of both, goodness knows!

"Last night they came into the parlour. Of course, in a night or two, they'll walk up into the bed-room.

MRS. CAUDLE VISITS THE KITCHEN—"MILLIONS OF BLACK-BEETLES!"

They'll be here—regiments of 'em—on the quilt. But what do you care? Nothing of the sort ever touches you: but you know how they come to me; and that's why you're so quiet. A pleasant thing to have black-beetles in one's bed! *Why don't I poison 'em?* A pretty matter, indeed, to have poison in the house! Much you must think of the dear children. A nice place too, to be called the Turtle-Dovery! *Didn't I christen it myself?* I know that—but then I knew nothing of the black-beetles. Besides, names of houses are for the world outside: not that anybody passes to see ours. Didn't Mrs. Digby insist on calling their new house 'Love-in-Idleness', though everybody knew that that wretch Digby was always beating her? Still, when folks read 'Rose Cottage' on the wall, they seldom think of the lots of thorns that are inside. In this world, Mr. Caudle, names are sometimes quite as good as things.

"That cough again! You've got a cold, and you'll always be getting one—for you'll always be missing the omnibus as you did on Tuesday—and always be getting wet. No constitution can stand it, Caudle. You don't know what I felt when I heard it rain on Tuesday, and thought you might be in it. What? *I'm very good?* Yes, I trust so: I try to be so, Caudle. And so, dear, I've been thinking that we'd better keep a chaise. *You can't afford it, and you won't?* Don't tell me: I know you'd save money by it. I've been reckoning what you lay out in omnibuses; and if you'd a chaise of your own—besides the gentility of the thing—you'd be money in pocket. And then again, how often I could go with you to town—and how, again, I could call for you when you liked to be a little late at the club, dear? Now, you're obliged to be hurried away, I know it, when, if you'd only a carriage of your own, you could stay and enjoy yourself. And after your work you want enjoyment. Of course, I can't expect you always to run home directly to me: and I don't, Caudle; and you know it.

"A nice, neat, elegant little chaise. What? *You'll think of it*? There's a love! You are a good creature, Caudle; and 'twill make me so happy to think you don't depend upon an omnibus. A sweet little carriage, with our arms beautifully painted on the panels. What? *Arms are rubbish; and you don't know that you have any*? Nonsense: to be sure you have—and if not, of course they're to be had for money. I wonder where Chalkpit's, the milkman's arms came from? I suppose you can buy 'em at the same place. He used to drive a green cart; and now he's got a close yellow carriage, with two large tortoise-shell cats, with their whiskers as if dipt in cream, standing on their hind legs upon each door, with a heap of Latin underneath. You may buy the carriage, if you please, Mr. Caudle; but unless your arms are there, you won't get me to enter it. Never! I'm not going to look less than Mrs. Chalkpit.

"Besides, if you hav'n't arms, I'm sure my family have, and a wife's arms are quite as good as a husband's. I'll write to-morrow to dear mother, to know what we took for our family arms. What do you say? What? *A mangle in a stone-kitchen proper*? Mr. Caudle, you're always insulting my family—always: but you shall not put me out of temper to-night. Still, if you don't like our arms, find your own. I dare say you could have found 'em fast enough, if you'd married Miss Prettyman. Well, I will be quiet; and I won't mention that lady's name. A nice lady she is! I wonder how much she spends in paint! Now, don't I tell you I won't say a word more; and yet you will kick about!

"Well, we'll have the carriage and the family arms? No, I don't want the family legs too. Don't be vulgar, Mr. Caudle. You might, perhaps, talk in that way before you'd money in the Bank; but it doesn't at all become you now. The carriage and the family arms! We've a country house as well as the Chalkpits; and though they praise their place for a little Paradise, I dare say they've quite as many black-beetles as we have, and more too. The place quite looks it.

"Our carriage and our arms! And you know, love, it won't cost much—next to nothing—to put a gold band about Sam's hat on a Sunday. No: I don't want a full-blown livery. At least, not just yet. I'm told the Chalkpits dress their boy on a Sunday like a dragon-fly: and I don't see why we shouldn't do what we like with our own Sam. Nevertheless, I'll be content with a gold band, and a bit of pepper-and-salt. No: I shall not cry out for plush next; certainly not. But I will have a gold band, and— *You won't; and I know it?* Oh yes! that's another of your crotchets, Mr. Caudle; like nobody else—you don't love liveries. I suppose when people buy their sheets, or their table cloths, or any other linen, they've a right to mark what they like upon it, haven't they? Well, then? You buy a servant, and you mark what you like upon him, and where's the difference? None, that I can see."

"Finally," says Caudle, "I compromised for a gig; but Sam did not wear pepper-and-salt and a gold band!"

Lecture XXXI

Mrs. Caudle Complains Very Bitterly that Mr. Caudle Has "Broken her Confidence"

"You'll catch me, Mr. Caudle, telling you anything again. Now, I don't want to have any noise: I don't wish you to put yourself in a passion. All I say is this; never again do I open my lips to you about anybody. No: if man and wife can't be one, why there's an end of everything. Oh, you know very well what I mean, Mr. Caudle: you've broken my confidence in the most shameful, the most heartless way, and I repeat it—I can never be again to you as I have been. No: the little charm—it wasn't much—that remained about married life, is gone for ever. Yes; the bloom's quite wiped off the plum now.

"Don't be such a hypocrite, Caudle; don't ask me what I mean. Mrs. Badgerly has been here—more like a fiend, I'm sure, than a quiet woman. I haven't done trembling yet! You know the state of my nerves, too; you know—yes, sir, I *had* nerves when you married me; and I haven't just found 'em out. Well, you've something to answer for, I think. The Badgerlys are going to separate: she takes the girls, and he the boys, and all through you. How you can lay your head upon that pillow and think of going to sleep, I can't tell. *What have you done?* Well, you have a face to ask the question. Done? You've

MR AND MRS. BADGERLY.

broken my confidence, Mr. Caudle: you've taken advantage of my tenderness, my trust in you as a wife— the more fool I for my pains?—and you've separated a happy couple for ever. No; I'm not talking in the clouds; I'm talking in your bed, the more my misfortune.

"Now, Caudle—yes, I shall sit up in the bed if I choose. I'm not going to sleep till I have this properly explained, for Mrs. Badgerly shan't lay her separation at my door. You won't deny that you were at the Club last night? No, bad as you are, Caudle—and though you're my husband, I can't think you a good man; I try to do, but I can't—bad as you are, you can't deny you were at the Club. What? *You don't deny it*? That's what I say—you can't. And now, answer me this question. What did you say—before the whole world—of Mr. Badgerly's whiskers? There's nothing to laugh at,

Caudle; if you'd have seen that poor woman, to-day, you'd have a heart of stone to laugh. What did you say of his whiskers? Didn't you tell everybody he dyed 'em? Didn't you hold the candle up to 'em, as you said, to show the purple? *To be sure you did*! Ha! people who break jokes never care about breaking hearts. Badgerly went home like a demon; called his wife a false woman: vowed he'd never enter a bed again with her, and, to show he was in earnest, slept all night upon the sofa. He said it was the dearest secret of his life; said she had told me; and that I had told you; and that's how it had come out. What do you say? *Badgerly was right? I did tell you?* I know I did: but when dear Mrs. Badgerly mentioned the matter to me and a few friends, as we were all laughing at tea together, quite in a confidential way— when she just spoke of her husband's whiskers, and how long he was over 'em every morning—of course, poor soul! she never thought it was to be talked of in the world again. Eh? *Then I had no right to tell you of it?* And that's the way I'm thanked for my confidence. Because I don't keep a secret from you, but show you, I may say, my naked soul, Caudle, that's how I'm rewarded. Poor Mrs. Badgerly—for all her hard words—after she went away, I'm sure my heart quite bled for her. What do you say, Mr. Caudle? *Serves her right—she should hold her tongue?* Yes; that's like your tyranny—you'd never let a poor woman speak. Eh—what, Mr. Caudle?

"That's a very fine speech, I dare say; and wives are very much obliged to you, only there's not a bit of truth in it. No, we women don't get together, and pick our husbands to pieces, just as sometimes mischievous little girls rip up their dolls. That's an old sentiment of yours, Mr. Caudle: but I'm sure you've no occasion to say it of me. I hear a good deal of other people's husbands, certainly; I can't shut my ears; I wish I could: but I never say anything about you—and I might, and you know it—and there's somebody else that knows it, too. No: I sit still and say nothing; what I have in my own bosom about you, Caudle, will be buried with me. But I know what you think of wives. I heard you talking to Mr. Prettyman, when you little thought I was listening, and you didn't know much what you were saying—I heard you. 'My dear Prettyman,' says you, 'when some women get talking, they club all their husbands' faults together; just as children club their cakes and apples, to make a common feast for the whole set.' Eh? *You don't remember it*? But I do: and I remember, too, what brandy was left, when Prettyman went. 'Twould be odd if you could remember much about it, after that.

"And now you've gone and separated man and wife, and I'm to be blamed for it. You've not only carried misery into a family, but broken my confidence. You've proved to me that henceforth I'm not to trust you with anything, Mr. Caudle. No: I'll lock up whatever I know in my own breast—for now I find nobody, not even one's own husband, is to be relied upon. From this moment, I may look upon myself as a solitary woman. Now it's no use your trying to go to sleep. What do you say? *You know that*? Very well. Now, I want to ask you one question more. Eh? *You want to ask me one*? Very well—go on—I'm not afraid to be catechised. I never dropt a syllable that as a wife I ought to have kept to myself—no, I'm not at all forgetting what I have said— and whatever you've got to ask me speak out at once. No—I don't want you to spare me; all I want you is to speak. You will speak? Well then, do.

"What? *Who told people you'd a false front tooth?* And is that all? Well, I'm sure—as if the world couldn't see it. I know I did just mention it once, but then I thought everybody knew it—besides, I was aggravated to do it; yes, aggravated. I remember it was that very day, at Mrs. Badgerly's when husbands' whiskers came up. Well, after we'd done with them, somebody said something about teeth. Whereupon, Miss Prettyman—a minx! she was born to destroy the peace of families, I know she was: she was there, and if I'd only known that such a creature was——no, I'm not rambling, not at all, and I'm coming to the tooth. To be sure, this is a great deal you've got against me, isn't it? Well, somebody spoke about teeth, when Miss Prettyman, with one of her insulting leers, said, 'She thought Mr. Caudle had the whitest teeth she ever *had* beheld.' Of course, my blood was up—every wife's would be: and I believe I might have said, 'Yes, they were well enough; but when a young lady so very much praised a married man's teeth, she perhaps didn't know that one of the front ones was an elephant's.' Like her impudence!—I set *her* down for the rest of the evening. But I can see the humour you're in to-night. You only came to bed to quarrel, and I'm not going to indulge you. All I say is this, after the shameful mischief you've made at the Badgerlys', you never break my confidence again. Never—and now you know it."

Caudle hereupon writes—"And here she seemed inclined to sleep. Not for one moment did I think to prevent her."

Lecture XXXII

Mrs. Caudle Discourses of Maids-of-all-Work and Maids in General. Mr. Caudle's "Infamous Behaviour" Ten Years Ago

"There now, it isn't my intention to say a word to-night, Mr. Caudle. No; I want to go to sleep, if I can; for after what I've gone through to-day, and with the head-ache I've got—and if I haven't left my smelling-salts on the mantelpiece, on the right-hand corner just as you go into the room—nobody could miss it—I say, nobody could miss it—in a little green bottle, and——well, there you lie like a stone, and I might perish and you wouldn't move. Oh, my poor head! But it may open and shut, and what do you care?

"Yes, that's like your feeling, just. I want my salts, and you tell me there's nothing like being still for a head-ache. Indeed? But I'm not going to be still; so don't you think it. That's just how a woman's put upon. But I know your aggravation—I know your art. You think to keep me quiet about that minx Kitty—your favourite, sir! Upon my life, I'm not to discharge my own servant without—but she shall go. If I had to do all the work myself, she shouldn't stop under my roof. I can see how she looks down upon me. I can see a great deal, Mr. Caudle, that I never choose to open my lips about—but I can't shut my eyes. Perhaps it would have been better for my peace of mind if I always could.

Don't say that. I'm not a foolish woman, and I know very well what I'm saying. I suppose you think I forget *that* Rebecca? I know it's ten years ago that she lived with us—but what's that to do with it? Things ar'n't the less true for being old, I suppose. No; and your conduct, Mr. Caudle, at that time —if it was a hundred years ago—I should never forget. *What? I shall always be the same silly woman?* I hope I shall—I trust I shall always have my eyes about me in my own house. Now, don't think of going to sleep, Caudle; because, as you've brought this up about that Rebecca, you shall hear me out. Well, I do wonder that you can name her! Eh? *You didn't name her?* That's nothing at all to do with it; for I know just as well what you think, as if you did. I suppose you'll say that you didn't drink a glass of wine to her? *Never?* So you said at the time, but I've thought of it for ten long years, and the more I've thought the surer I am of it. And at that very time—if you please to recollect—at that very time little Jack was a baby. I shouldn't have so much cared but for that; but he was hardly running alone, when you nodded and drank a glass of wine to that creature. No; I'm not mad, and I'm not dreaming. I saw how you did it—and the hypocrisy made it worse and worse. I saw you when the creature was just behind my chair, you took up a glass of wine, and saying to me, 'Margaret', and then lifting up your eyes at the bold minx, and saying, 'my dear', as if you wanted me to believe that you spoke only to me, when I could see you laugh at her behind me. And at that time little Jack wasn't on his feet. What do you say? *Heaven forgive me?* Ha! Mr. Caudle, it's you who ought to ask for that: I'm safe enough, I am: it's you who should ask to be forgiven.

"No, I wouldn't slander a saint—and I didn't take

"YOU NODDED AND DRANK A GLASS OF WINE TO THAT
CREATURE."

away the girl's character for nothing. I know she
brought an action for what I said; and I know you had to
pay damages for what you call my tongue—I well
remember all that. And serve you right; if you hadn't
laughed at her, it wouldn't have happened. But if you
will make free with such people, of course you're sure to
suffer for it. 'Twould have served you right if the
lawyer's bill had been double. Damages, indeed! Not
that anybody's tongue could have damaged her!

"And now, Mr. Caudle, you're the same man you were
ten years ago. What? *You hope so?* The more shame for
you. At your time of life, with all your children growing
up about you, to—*What am I talking of?* I know very

well; and so would you, if you had any conscience, which you haven't. When I say I shall discharge Kitty, you say she's a very good servant, and I shan't get a better. But I know why you think her good; you think her pretty, and that's enough for you; as if girls who work for their bread have any business to be pretty—which she isn't. Pretty servants, indeed! going mincing about with their fal-lal faces, as if even the flies would spoil 'em. But I know what a bad man you are—now, it's no use your denying it; for didn't I overhear you talking to Mr. Prettyman, and didn't you say that you couldn't bear to have ugly servants about you? I ask you—didn't you say that? *Perhaps you did?* You don't blush to confess it? If your principles, Mr. Caudle, ar'n't enough to make a woman's blood run cold!

"Oh, yes! you've talked that stuff again and again; and once I might have believed it; but I know a little more of you now. You like to see pretty servants, just as you like to see pretty statues, and pretty pictures, and pretty flowers, and anything in nature that's pretty, just, as you say, for the eye to feed upon. Yes; I know your eyes—very well, I know what they were ten years ago; for shall I ever forget that glass of wine when little Jack was in arms? I don't care if it was a thousand years ago, it's as fresh as yesterday, and I never will cease to talk of it. When you know me, how can you ask it?

"And now you insist upon keeping Kitty, when there's no having a bit of crockery for her? That girl would break the Bank of England—I know she would —if she was to put her hand upon it. But what's a whole set of blue china to her beautiful blue eyes? I know that's what you mean, though you don't say it.

"Oh, you needn't lie groaning there, for you don't

think I shall ever forget Rebecca. Yes—it's very well for you to swear at Rebecca now—but you didn't swear at her then, Mr. Caudle, I know. 'Margaret my dear!' Well, how you can have the face to look at me—*You don't look at me?* The more shame for you.

"I can only say, that either Kitty leaves the house, or I do. Which is it to be, Mr. Caudle? Eh? *You don't care? Both?* But you're not going to get rid of me in that manner, I can tell you. But for that trollop—now you may swear and rave as you like—*You don't intend to say a word more?* Very well; it's no matter what you say—her quarter's up on Tuesday, and go she shall. A soup-plate and a basin went yesterday.

"A soup-plate and a basin, and when I've the headache as I have, Mr. Caudle, tearing me to pieces! But I shall never be well in this world—never. A soup-plate and a basin!"

MRS. CAUDLE DISCHARGES "KITTY".

185

"She slept," writes Caudle, "and poor Kitty left on Tuesday."

Lecture XXXIII

Mrs. Caudle Has Discovered that Caudle Is a Railway Director

"When I took up the paper to-day, Caudle, you might have knocked me down with a feather! Now, don't be a hypocrite—you know what's the matter. And when you haven't a bed to lie upon, and are brought to sleep upon coal-sacks—and then I can tell you, Mr. Caudle, you may sleep by yourself—then you'll know what's the matter. Now, I've seen your name, and don't deny it. Yes—the Eel-Pie Island Railway—and among the Directors, Job Caudle, Esq., of the Turtle-Dovery, and—no, I won't be quiet. It isn't often—goodness knows!—that I speak; but seeing what I do, I won't be silent. *What do I see?* Why, there, Mr. Caudle, at the foot of the bed, I see all the blessed children in tatters—I see you in a gaol, and the carpets hung out at the windows.

"And now I know why you talk in your sleep about a broad and narrow gauge! I couldn't think what was on your mind—but now it's out. Ha! Mr. Caudle, there's something about a broad and narrow way that I wish you'd remember—but you're turned quite a heathen: yes, you think of nothing but money now. *Don't I like money?* To be sure I do; but then I like it when I'm certain of it; no risks for me. Yes, it's all very well to talk about fortunes made in no time: they're like shirts made in no time—it's ten to one if they hang long together.

"And now it's plain enough why you can't eat or drink, or sleep, or do anything. All your mind's allotted into railways; for you shan't make me believe that Eel-Pie Island's the only one. Oh no! I can see by the looks of you. Why, in a little time, if you haven't as many lines in your face as there are lines laid down! Every one of your features seems cut up—and all seem travelling from one another. Six months ago, Caudle, you hadn't a wrinkle; yes, you'd a cheek as smooth as any china, and now your face is like the Map of England.

"At your time of life, too! You, who were for always going small and sure! You to make heads and tails of your money in this way! It's that stockbroker's dog at Flam Cottage—he's bitten you, I'm sure of it. You're not fit to manage your own property now; and I should

MR. CAUDLE READS THE SHARE-LIST.

be only acting the part of a good wife, if I were to call in the mad doctors.

"Well, I shall never know rest any more now. There won't be a soul knock at the door after this, that I shan't think it's the man coming to take possession. 'Twill be something for the Chalkpits to laugh at when we're sold up. I think I see 'em here, bidding for all our little articles of bigotry and virtue, and—what are you laughing at? *They're not bigotry and virtue; but bijouterie and vertu?* It's all the same: only you're never so happy as when you're taking me up.

"If I can tell what's come to the world, I'm a sinner! Everybody's for turning their farthings into double sovereigns, and cheating their neighbours of the balance. And you, too—you're beside yourself, Caudle— I'm sure of it. I've watched you when you thought me fast asleep. And then you've lain, and whispered and whispered, and then hugged yourself, and laughed at the bed-posts, as if you'd seen 'em turned to sovereign gold. I do believe that you sometimes think the patch-work quilt is made of thousand-pound bank-notes.

"Well, when we're brought to the Union, then you'll find out your mistake. But it will be a poor satisfaction for me every night to tell you of it. What, Mr. Caudle? *They won't let me tell you of it?* And you call that 'some comfort?' And after the wife I've been to you! But now I recollect. I think I've heard you praise that Union before; though, like a fond fool as I've always been, I never once suspected the reason of it.

"And now, of course, day and night you'll never be at home? No, you'll live and sleep at Eel-Pie Island! I shall be left alone with nothing but my thoughts, thinking when the broker will come, and you'll be with your brother directors. I may slave and I may toil to save sixpences; and you'll be throwing away hundreds. And then the expensive tastes you've got! Nothing good enough for you now. I'm sure you sometimes think yourself King Solomon. But that comes of making money—if, indeed, you have made any—without earning it. No: I don't talk nonsense: people *can* make money without earning it. And when they do, why it's like taking a lot of spirits at one draught; it gets into their head, and they don't know what they're about. And you're in that state now, Mr. Caudle: I'm sure of it by the way of you. There's a tipsiness of the pocket as well as of the stomach—and you're in that condition at this very moment.

"Not that I should so much mind—that is, if you *have* made money—if you'd stop at the Eel-Pie line. But I know what these things are: they're like treacle to flies: when men are well in 'em, they can't get out of 'em: or if they do, it's often without a feather to fly with. No: if you've really made money by the Eel-Pie line, and will give it to me to take care of for the dear children, why, perhaps, love, I'll say no more of the matter. What! *Nonsense?* Yes, of course: I never ask you for money, but that's the word.

"And now, catching you stopping at the Eel-Pie line! Oh, no, I know your aggravating spirit. In a day or two I shall see another fine flourish in the paper, with a proposal for a branch from Eel-Pie Island to the Chelsea Bun-house. Give you a mile of rail, and—I know you men—you'll take a hundred. Well, if it didn't make me quiver to read that stuff in the paper—and your name to it! But I suppose it was Mr. Prettyman's work; for his precious name's among 'em. How you tell the people 'that eel-pies are now become an essential element of civilisation'—I learnt all the words by heart, that I might say 'em to you—'that the Eastern population of London are cut off from the blessings of such a necessary—and that by means of the projected line eel-pies will be brought home to the business and bosoms of Ratcliffe-highway, and the adjacent dependencies.' Well when you men—lords of the creation, as you call yourselves—do get together to make up a company, or anything of the sort—is there any story-book can come up to you? And so you look solemnly in one another's faces, and never so much as moving the corners of your mouths, pick one another's pockets. No! I'm not using hard words, Mr. Caudle—but only the words that's proper.

"And this I *must* say. Whatever you've got, I'm none the better for it. You never give me any of your Eel-Pie shares. What do you say? *You will give me some?* Not I—I'll not have nothing to do with any wickedness of the kind. If, like any other husband, you choose to throw a heap of money into my lap—what? *You'll think of it? When the Eel-Pies go up?* Then I know what they're worth—they'll never fetch a farthing."

"She was suddenly silent"—writes Caudle—"and I was sinking into sleep, when she elbowed me, and cried, 'Caudle, do you think they'll be up to-morrow?'"

LECTURE XXXIV

Mrs. Caudle, Suspecting that Mr. Caudle Has Made his Will, Is "Only Anxious as a Wife" to Know its Provisions

"I always said you'd a strong mind when you liked, Caudle; and what you've just been doing proves it. Some people won't make a will, because they think they must die directly afterwards. Now, you're above that love, ar'n't you? Nonsense; you know very well what I mean. I know your will's made, for Scratcherly told me so. What? *You don't believe it*? Well, I'm sure! That's a pretty thing for a man to say to his wife. I know he's too much a man of business to talk; but I suppose there's a way of telling things without speaking them. And when I put the question to him, lawyer as he is, he hadn't the face to deny it.

"To be sure, it can be of no consequence to me whether your will is made or not. I shall not be alive, Mr. Caudle, to want anything: I shall be provided for a long time before your will's of any use. No, Mr. Caudle; I shan't survive you: and—though a woman's wrong to let her affection for a man be known, for then she's always taken advantage of—though I know it's foolish and weak to say so, still I don't want to survive you. How should I? No, no: don't say that: I'm not good for a hundred—I shan't see you out, and another husband too. What a gross idea, Caudle! To imagine I'd ever

193

"LAWYER AS HE IS, HE HADN'T THE FACE TO DENY IT."

think of marrying again. No—never! What? *That's what we all say?* Not at all; quite the reverse. To me the very idea of such a thing is horrible, and always was. Yes, I know very well that some do marry again—but what they're made of, I'm sure I can't tell.—Ugh!

"There are men, I know, who leave their property in such a way that their widows, to hold it, must keep widows. Now, if there is anything in the world that is mean and small, it is that. Don't you think so too, Caudle? Why don't you speak, love? That's so like you! I never want a little quiet rational talk, but you want to go to sleep. But you never were like any other man! What? *How do I know?* There now—that's so like your aggravating way. I never open my lips upon a subject, but you try to put me off. I've no doubt when Miss Prettyman speaks, you can answer *her* properly enough. There you are, again! Upon my life, it *is* odd; but I never can in the most innocent way mention that person's name that—*Why can't I leave her alone?* I'm sure—with all my heart! Who wants to talk about her? I don't: only you always will say something that's certain to bring up her name.

"What was I saying, Caudle? Oh, about the way some men bind their widows. To my mind, there is nothing so little. When a man forbids his wife to marry again without losing what he leaves—it's what I call selfishness after death. Mean to a degree! It's like taking his wife into the grave with him. Eh? *You never want to do that?* No, I'm sure of that, love: you're not the man to tie a woman up in that mean manner. A man who'd do that, would have his widow burnt with him, if he could—just as those monsters, that call themselves men, do in the Indies.

"However, it's no matter to me how you've made your will; but it may be to your second wife. What? *I shall never give you a chance?* Ha! you don't know my constitution after all, Caudle. I'm not at all the woman I was. I say nothing about 'em, but very often you don't know my feelings. And as we're on the subject, dearest, I have only one favour to ask. When you marry again— now it's no use your saying that. After the comforts you've known of marriage—what are you sighing at, dear?—after the comforts, you must marry again.—Now don't forswear yourself in that violent way, taking an oath

195

that you know you must break—you couldn't help it, I'm sure of it; and I know you better than you know yourself. Well, all I ask is, love, because it's only for your sake, and it would make no difference to me then—how should it?—but all I ask is, don't marry Miss Pret——There! there! I've done; I won't say another word about it; but all I ask is, don't. After the way you've been thought of, and after the comforts you've been used to, Caudle, she wouldn't be the wife for you. Of course, I could then have no interest in the matter—you might marry the Queen of England, for what it would be to me then—I'm only anxious about you. Mind, Caudle, I'm not saying anything against her; not at all; but there's a flightiness in her manner—I dare say, poor thing, she means no harm, and it may be, as the saying is, only her manner after all—still, there *is* a flightiness about her that, after what you've been used to, would make you very wretched. Now, if I may boast of anything, Caudle, it is my propriety of manner the whole of my life. I know that wives who're very particular, ar'n't thought as well of as those who're not—still, it's next to nothing to be virtuous, if people don't seem so. And virtue, Caudle— no, I'm not going to preach about virtue, for I never do. No; and I don't go about with my virtue, like a child with a drum, making all sorts of noises with it. But I know your principles. I shall never forget what I once heard you say to Prettyman: and it's no excuse that you'd taken so much wine you didn't know what you were saying at the time; for wine brings out men's wickedness, just as fire brings out spots of grease. *What did you say?* Why you said this:—'Virtue's a beautiful thing in women, when they don't make so much noise about it; but there's some women, who think virtue was given to 'em, as claws were given to cats'—yes, cats was the word—'to do nothing but scratch with.' That's what you said. *You don't recollect a syllable of it?* No, that's it; when you're in that dreadful state, you recollect nothing: but it's a good thing I do.

"But we won't talk of that, love—that's all over: I dare say you meant nothing. But I'm glad you agree with me, that the man who'd tie up his widow, not to marry again, is a mean man. It makes me happy that you've that confidence in me to say that. *You never said it?* That's nothing to do with it—you've just as good as said it. No: when a man leaves all his property to his wife, without binding her hands from marrying again, he shows what a dependence he has upon her love. He proves to all the world what a wife she's been to him; and how, after his death, he knows she'll grieve for him. And then, of course, a second marriage never enters her head. But when she only keeps his money so long as she keeps a widow, why she's aggravated to take another husband. I'm sure of it; many a poor woman has been driven into wedlock again, only because she was spited into it by her husband's will. It's only natural to suppose it. If I thought, Caudle, you could do such a thing, though it would break my heart to do it—yet, though you were dead and gone, I'd show you I'd a spirit, and marry again directly. Not but what it's ridiculous my talking in such a way, as I shall go long before you; still, mark my words, and don't provoke me with any will of that sort, or I'd do it—as I'm a living woman in this bed tonight, I'd do it."

"I did not contradict her," says Caudle, "but suffered her to slumber in such assurance."

Lecture XXXV

Mrs. Caudle "Has Been Told" that Caudle Has "Taken to Play" at Billiards

"You're very late to-night, dear. *It's not late?* Well, then, it isn't, that's all. Of course, a woman can never tell when it's late. You were late on Tuesday, too: a little late on the Friday before; on the Wednesday before that—now, you needn't twist about in that manner; I'm not going to say anything—no; for I see it's now no use. Once, I own, it used to fret me when you stayed out; but that's all over: you've now brought me to that state, Caudle—and it's your own fault, entirely—that I don't care whether you ever come home or not. I never thought I could be brought to think so little of you; but you've done it: you've been treading on the worm for these twenty years, and it's turned at last.

"Now, I'm not going to quarrel; that's all over: I don't feel enough for you to quarrel with—I don't, Caudle, as true as I'm in this bed. All I want of you is—any other man would speak to his wife, and not lie there like a log—all I want is this. Just tell me where you were on Tuesday? You were not at dear mother's, though you know she's not well, and you know she thinks of leaving the dear children her money; but you never had any feeling for anybody belonging to me. And you were not at your Club: no, I know that. And you were not at any theatre. *How do I know?* Ha, Mr. Caudle! I only wish I didn't know. No; you were not at any of these places; but I know well enough where you were. *Then why do I ask if I know?* That's it: just to prove what a hypocrite you are: just to show you that you can't deceive me.

"So, Mr. Caudle—you've turned billiard-player, sir. *Only once?* That's quite enough: you might as well play a thousand times; for you're a lost man, Caudle. Only once, indeed. I wonder, if I was to say 'Only once', what would you say to me? But, of course, a man can do no wrong in anything.

"And you're a lord of the creation, Mr. Caudle; and you can stay away from the comforts of your blessed fireside, and the society of your own wife and children—though, to be sure, you never thought anything of them—to push ivory balls about with a long stick upon a green table-cloth. What pleasure any man

MR. CAUDLE "TAKES TO BILLIARDS".

can take in such stuff must astonish any sensible woman. I pity you, Caudle!

"And you can go and do nothing but make 'cannons'—for that's the gibberish they talk at billiards—when there's the manly and athletic game of cribbage, as my poor grand-mother used to call it, at your own hearth. You can go into a billiard-room—you, a respectable tradesman, or as you set yourself up for one, for if the world knew all, there's very little respectability in you—you can go and play billiards with a set of creatures in mustachios, when you might take a nice, quiet hand with me at home. But no! anything but cribbage with your own wife!

"Caudle, it's all over now; you've gone to destruction. I never knew a man enter a billiard-room that he wasn't lost for ever. There was my uncle Wardle; a better man never broke the bread of life; he took to billiards, and he didn't live with aunt a month afterwards. *A lucky fellow?* And that's what you call a man who leaves his wife—a 'lucky fellow?' But, to be sure, what can I expect? We shall not be together long, now: it's been some time coming, but, at last, we must separate: and the wife I've been to you!

"But I know who it is; it's that fiend, Prettyman. I *will* call him a fiend, and I'm by no means a foolish woman: you'd no more have thought of billiards than a goose, if it hadn't been for him. Now, it's no use, Caudle, your telling me that you have only been once, and that you can't hit a ball anyhow—you'll soon get over all that; and then you'll never be at home. You'll be a marked man, Caudle; yes, marked: there'll be something about you that'll be dreadful; for if I couldn't tell a billiard-player by his looks, I've no eyes, that's all. They all of 'em look as yellow as parchment, and wear mustachios—I suppose you'll let yours grow, now; though they'll be a good deal troubled to come, I know that. Yes, they've all a yellow and sly look; just for all as if they were first-cousins to people that picked pockets. And that will be your case, Caudle: in six months, the dear children won't know their own father.

"Well, if I know myself at all, I could have borne anything but billiards. The companions you'll find. The Captains that will be always borrowing fifty pounds of you! I tell you, Caudle, a billiard-room's a place where ruin of all sorts is made easy, I may say, to the lowest understanding—so you can't miss it. It's a chapel of ease for the devil to preach in—don't tell me not to be eloquent: I don't know what you mean, Mr. Caudle, and I shall be just as eloquent as I like. But I never can open my lips—and it isn't often, goodness knows!—that I'm not insulted.

"No, I won't be quiet on this matter; I won't, Caudle: on any other, I wouldn't say a word—and you know it— if you didn't like it; but on this matter, I *will* speak. I know you can't play at billiards; and never could learn—I dare say not; but that makes it all the worse, for look at the money you'll lose; see the ruin you'll be brought to. It's no use your telling me you'll not play— now you can't help it. And nicely you'll be eaten up. Don't talk to me; dear aunt told me all about it. The lots of fellows that go every day into billiard-rooms to get their dinners, just as a fox sneaks into a farm-yard to look about him for a fat goose—and they'll eat you up, Caudle; I know they will.

"Billiard-balls, indeed! Well, in my time, I've been over Woolwich Arsenal—you were something like a man then, for it was just before we were married—and then, I saw all sorts of balls; mountains of 'em, to be shot away at churches, and into people's peaceable habitations, breaking the china, and nobody knows what—I say, I've seen all these balls—well, I know I've said that before; but I choose to say it again—and there's not one of 'em, iron as they are, that could do half the mischief of a billiard-ball. That's a ball, Caudle, that's gone through many a wife's heart, to say nothing of her children. And that's a ball, that night and day you'll be destroying your family with. Don't tell me you'll not play! When once a man's given to it—as my poor aunt used to say—the devil's always tempting him with a ball, as he tempted Eve with an apple.

"I shall never think of being happy any more. No: that's quite out of the question. You'll be there every night—I know you will, better than you, so don't deny it—every night over that wicked green cloth. Green, indeed! It's red, crimson red, Caudle, if you could only properly see it—crimson red, with the hearts those balls have broken. Don't tell me not to be pathetic—I shall: as pathetic as it suits me. I suppose I may speak. However, I've done. It's all settled now. You're a billiard player, and I'm a wretched woman."

"I did not deny either position," writes Caudle, "and for this reason—I wanted to sleep."

Mrs. Caudle Has Taken Cold; The Tragedy of Thin Shoes

"I'm not going to contradict you, Caudle; you may say what you like—but I think I ought to know my own feelings better than you. I don't wish to upbraid you neither; I'm too ill for that; but it's not getting wet in thin shoes—oh, no! it's my mind, Caudle, my mind, that's killing me. Oh, yes! gruel, indeed—you think gruel will cure a woman of anything; and you know, too, how I hate it. Gruel can't reach what I suffer; but, of course, nobody is ever ill but yourself. Well, I—I didn't mean to say that; but when you talk in that way about thin shoes, a woman says, of course, what she doesn't mean; she can't help it. You've always gone on about my shoes; when I think I'm the fittest judge of what becomes me best. I dare say—'twould be all the same to you if I put on ploughman's boots; but I'm not going to make a figure of my feet, I can tell you. I've never got cold with the shoes I've worn yet, and 'tisn't likely I should begin now.

"No, Caudle; I wouldn't wish to say anything to accuse you; no, goodness knows, I wouldn't make you uncomfortable for the world—but the cold I've got, I got ten years ago. I have never said anything about it—but it has never left me. Yes; ten years ago the day before yesterday. *How can I recollect it?* Oh, very well: women remember things you never think of: poor souls! they've good cause to do so. Ten years ago, I was sitting up for you—there now, I'm not going to say anything to vex you, only do let me speak: ten years ago, I was waiting for you—and I fell asleep, and the fire went out, and when I woke I found I was sitting right in the draught of the key-hole. That was my death, Caudle, though don't let that make you uneasy, love; for I don't think you meant to do it.

"Ha! it's all very well for you to call it nonsense; and to lay your ill conduct upon my shoes. That's like a man, exactly! There never was a man yet that killed his wife, who couldn't give a good reason for it. No: I don't mean to say that you've killed me: quite the reverse: still, there's never been a day that I haven't felt that key-hole. What? *Why won't I have a doctor?* What's the use of a doctor? Why should I put you to expense? Besides, I dare say you'll do very well without me, Caudle: yes, after a very little time, you won't miss me much—no man ever does.

"Peggy tells me, Miss Prettyman called to-day. *What of it?* Nothing, of course. Yes; I know she heard I was ill, and that's why she came. A little indecent, I think, Mr. Caudle; she might wait; I shan't be in her way long; she may soon have the key of the caddy, now.

"Ha! Mr. Caudle, what's the use of your calling me your dearest soul now? Well, I do believe you. I dare say you do mean it; that is, I hope you do. Nevertheless, you can't expect I can lie quiet in this bed, and think of that young woman—not, indeed, that she's near so young as she gives herself out. I bear no malice towards her, Caudle—not the least. Still, I don't think I could lay at peace in my grave if—well, I won't say anything more about her; but you know what I mean.

"I think dear mother would keep house beautifully for you, when I'm gone. Well, love, I won't talk in that way if you desire it. Still, I know I've a dreadful cold; though I won't allow it for a minute to be the shoes— certainly not. I never would wear 'em thick, and you know it, and they never gave me cold yet. No, dearest Caudle, it's ten years ago that did it; not that I'll say a syllable of the matter to hurt you. I'd die first.

"Mother, you see, knows all your little ways; and you wouldn't get another wife to study you and pet you up as I've done—a second wife never does; it isn't likely she should. And after all, we've been very happy. It hasn't been my fault, if we've ever had a word or two, for you couldn't help now and then being aggravating; nobody can help their tempers always—especially men. Still we've been very happy, haven't we, Caudle?

"Good night. Yes—this cold does tear me to pieces; but for all that, it isn't the shoes. God bless you, Caudle; no—it's *not* the shoes. I won't say it's the key-hole; but again I say, it's not the shoes. God bless you once more—But never say it's the shoes."

The significant sketch is on the previous page is a correct copy of a drawing from the hand of Caudle at the end of this Lecture. It can hardly, we think, be imagined that Mrs. Caudle, during her fatal illness, never mixed admon-ishment with soothing as before; but such fragmentary Lectures were, doubtless, considered by her discon-solate widower as having too touching, too solemn an import to be vulgarised by type. They were, however, printed on the heart of Caudle; for he never ceased to speak of the late partner of his bed but as either "his sainted creature", or "that angel now in heaven".

MR. CAUDLE A WIDOWER.

Postscript

Our duty of editorship is closed. We hope we have honestly fulfilled the task of selection from a large mass of papers. We could have presented to the female world a Lecture for Every Night in the Year. Yes—three hundred and sixty-five separate Lectures! We trust, however, that we have done enough. And if we have armed weak woman with even one argument in her unequal contest with that imperious creature, man—if we have awarded to a sex, as Mrs. Caudle herself was wont to declare, "put upon from the beginning", the slightest means of defence—if we have supplied a solitary text to meet any one of the manifold wrongs with which woman, in her household life, is continually pressed by her tyrannic task-master, man—we feel that we have only paid back one grain, hardly one, of that mountain of more than gold it is our felicity to owe her.

During the progress of these Lectures, it has very often pained us, and that excessively, to hear from unthinking, inexperienced men—bachelors of course —that every woman, no matter how divinely composed, has in her ichor-flowing veins, one drop—"no bigger than a wren's eye"—of Caudle; that Eve herself may now and then have been guilty of a lecture, murmuring it balmily amongst the rose-leaves.

It may be so; still, be it our pride never to believe it. NEVER!

The end of Mrs. Caudle's Curtain Lectures.